THE FARMERS' MARKET COOKBOOK

NINA PLANCK

PHOTOGRAPHS BY SARAH CUTTLE

Hodder & Stoughton

For Stephen, who ate everything

Thanks to: Julia Hobsbawm and Felicity Rubinstein for making this book happen; Marion McGilvary for the cook's journal, which saved me from drowning in bits of paper; Margaret Ferrazzi for her fajita, braised cabbage, and roast beef recipes, and for lots of hard work and good advice; Charlotte Deme, Peter Gordon, and the chefs at the *Duke of Cambridge*, *Restaurant Nora*, the *River Café*, and *Moro* for sharing recipes; Hazel Orme and Karen Sullivan for hundreds of improvements large and small; Cheryl Cohen, for remaining unruffled while doing the work of two people; Peter Clarke, Heidi Fermor, David Deme, and other farmers who corrected many mistakes (any remaining are mine alone); Angela Herlihy for wise and sensitive editing; and to Alasdair Oliver and Sarah Cuttle, who made this book more beautiful than I ever imagined.

Many thanks to the farmers who have worked at all hours, in all weather, all year long to bring beautiful, fresh food to towns and cities all over Britain. Special thanks to the original farmers at the Islington Farmers' Market for taking a chance on a somewhat keen American with an idea.

I am most grateful to my parents, Chip and Susan, for raising three kids on simple, home-grown food. Mom, thank you for leaving behind hundreds of little pepper plants for a last-minute trip to England. No one else could get the pies right. And Dad – thanks for watering the peppers.

Design Alasdair Oliver   Photography Sarah Cuttle

Copyright © 2001 by Nina Planck

First published in Great Britain in 2001 by Hodder and Stoughton
A division of Hodder Headline

The right of Nina Planck to be identified as the Author of the Work has been asserted by her in accordance with the Copyright, Designs and Patents Act 1988.

10 9 8 7 6 5 4 3 2 1

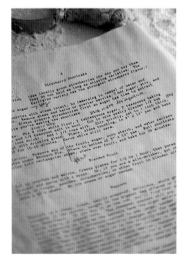

British Library Cataloguing in Publication Data

Planck, Nina
    The farmers' market cookbook
    1.Cookery
    I. Title
    641.5

ISBN 0 340 76847 9

Printed and bound in Great Britain by Butler & Tanner, Frome.

Hodder and Stoughton
A division of Hodder Headline
338 Euston Road
London NW1 3BH

FOREWORD

I like to know what I'm putting in my mouth. But modern food shopping is a minefield. We have learned the hard way to mistrust factory farming and agri-business. Food additives confuse us. We are suspicious of the motives of supermarkets. The natural seasons of fruit and vegetables are blurred. Our food is anonymous, its provenance distant, its background mysterious.

Who knew, until the BSE disaster unfolded, that farmers were feeding sheep brains to cattle, turning a natural herbivore into a carnivore? Did anyone tell us that most lettuce has been sprayed a dozen times? Or that the flood of cheap imported plums has nearly wiped out our own orchards, along with countless traditional varieties?

If you are curious about such things, greengrocers and supermarket managers are little help. Most haven't a clue what variety of peas or carrots they are selling. Potatoes are Jerseys, Cyprus, or Baking. Plums are Spanish, Victoria, or South African. They can't say whether the strawberries were grown outdoors or in poly-tunnels, or what they were sprayed with. They know the french beans are from Zimbabwe – it says so on the box – but little else.

There is a better way to shop. A way that restores not only character but flavour to the food. A way that is a pleasure, rather than a chore. My first trip to a farmers' market was a revelation. The farmer described his apple varieties – when he had picked them, which were at their peak, why I couldn't buy the ones I wanted (they would have a richer flavour if left on the tree a bit longer). Best of all, I sampled all the varieties with a pen knife.

So I was glad when Nina chose my neighbourhood for her farmers' market. I'm now a regular at the Islington market on Sunday mornings. When the bell rings at 10 o'clock (okay, so I'm not often there at the bell), I can buy baby greens only hours old, fresh Cromer crab, wild damsons, unfiltered honey, grass-fed lamb, organic eggs. There are strawberries on the plant and Brussels sprouts on the stalk. The food is fresh, seasonal, and locally grown. I can ask all the questions I want. What better way to know what I am putting in my mouth?

Nigel Slater
London, August 2000

WHEATLAND, VIRGINIA

What was paradise, but a garden full of vegetables and herbs and pleasure?
Nothing there but delights.

William Lawson, 17th century

I grew up on a 60-acre farm in Wheatland, Virginia. The first summer we farmed, we sold our fruit and vegetables by the side of the road in nearby small towns. We didn't sell much. The following summer, the first farmers' markets opened in Greater Washington, DC, about an hour's drive away. The first time we went to market, in 1980, we picked beetroots and Swiss chard at six a.m. and turned up an hour late.

We were amazed. It was as if the customers had waited all their lives to buy fresh produce in a car park on Saturday morning. Word spread, and the markets grew. Now my parents sell at fifteen farmers' markets a week in peak season. You have to go where the people are.

We could not have made a living farming without farmers' markets. But there is more to markets than money. It is deeply gratifying to sell food you have grown to people who appreciate it. The customers' delight makes all the hoeing, mulching, and picking worthwhile. Going to market with a truck full of produce and coming home with empty baskets is fun, too.

Work or pleasure, farm life revolved around fruit and vegetables. They mark the seasons; May means strawberries, October pumpkins. They set the agenda: when the pepper seedlings got big, it was time to transplant. Naturally produce played a major role in the kitchen. We ate home-grown food at every meal. My father calls it a vegetable-driven existence.

When I was growing up, we started work at six a.m. with the corn pick. We picked in the cold dew because heat quickly turns the sugars in sweetcorn to starch. Besides, dry corn leaves are like razors. At age ten, I was thrilled to be a corn-picker, because judging ripeness is tricky. If the ear is immature, the kernels are small and insipid. If it is over-ripe, they are tough and starchy. A good corn-picker picks by feel, never opening the husk.

The sky would be brilliant pink as we drove the wagon to the patch and plunged into the cold, wet arches. It was a harsh way to wake up, but after a while I liked being wet to my skin. I carried a tall basket under my left arm and groped for each ear with my right hand. When the ear felt perfect, I snapped it off in one quick motion. Snap, clunk, snap, clunk, snap, clunk, the heavy ears fell into the basket. I bent a green stalk to mark my place, dumped my basket on the wagon, and filled it again. On the way back to the house, I was the Corn Queen, bouncing on a load of slippery ears. Now the sun was high, and it drew a strong smell from our clothes. It was sweet, like evaporating corn syrup, and made me hungry. Breakfast was three ears each, boiled for just three minutes, with butter, salt, and pepper.

The squash and cucumber pick was less exciting. It was hot and the stems are spiny. But courgettes and yellow squashes are beautiful plants. Orange, trumpet-like flowers shudder and buzz. They are full of bees. Squash grows fast in hot weather: one day it is too young, the next it is the right size, and a day later, too big. If you miss a courgette for several days after its tender prime, it becomes dull and tough – a marrow. We called them zucchini baseball bats and fed them to the cow.

At midday we took a three-hour break. In high summer, Virginia is like a Turkish bath. During a heatwave, the sky is white and cloudless. There is no breeze; your skin prickles with sweat. The hours between noon and three o'clock are no time to pick okra, another scratchy plant.

It was time to eat. Lunch was usually tomato sandwiches and leftovers – summer squash and cheese, garlicky french beans, cold peach pie. After lunch we met under the ash tree for more work: hoeing and mulching in June, picking tomatoes, melons, peppers in August. If you were going to market the next day, you would load the truck, bunch basil, write signs. By eight or nine o'clock, depending on the day and season, work was done. Only then did we think about dinner.

The pace of farm life influenced how we ate, and what we believed to be good cooking. Above all, good cooking meant using our own fruit and vegetables. That was easy; we simply ate what was in season, what came back from market, what grew near the house, what was fresh. Sometimes we ate the very first peas or strawberries ourselves. More often we took them to market and waited for the surplus.

Good cooking meant quick, unfussy food with few ingredients and simple flavours. In a restaurant, if I ask my father how he finds the pumpkin risotto, he will often say, 'It's nice, but I can't taste the pumpkin.' I like to taste the undisguised essence of vegetables and fruit. They need very little.

Good cooking meant eating well in two senses: food that was not only healthy but delicious. It meant using whole, fresh, unsprayed foods as much as possible. It didn't mean fat-free spa menus. Hard work gave us big appetites, and good fats – cold-pressed vegetable oils, real butter, fish oils, untreated meats – are good for you anyway. We liked food you could eat a lot of, every day, and live long and happy. I still cook and eat that way.

When I visit the farm now, I don't work much. I prefer to be in the kitchen. I am still awed by the array of fresh fruit and vegetables – nothing there but delights. On the south wall of the kitchen, under the window and out of the sun, are baskets of tomatoes, aubergines, and peppers, sweet and hot. There is a ceramic bowl of home-grown garlic. In the freezer we keep sugared strawberries, whole blueberries, *Garden Salsa* chillies, and Italian frying peppers. Sometimes there are yellow and red bottled tomatoes. We eat them straight from the jar in the winter, with a big bowl of hot popcorn tossed with olive oil and ground cayenne.

The chickens are free to forage on insects and weeds, so our eggs have deep yellow yolks. For years we drank rich milk from our Jersey, Mabel. I hated smelling of cow when I had to milk before school. Eventually we lured Mabel into a truck with a bushel of corn, and sold her. It seems sad now.

The real bounty is outside, most of it a short walk from the house. In the dead of winter, we can grow salad leaves in the greenhouse. It takes a few minutes to fill a large bowl. In March, curly spinach planted in September comes back to life. In April and May, the greenhouse is filled with annual herbs, including purple, cinnamon, Genovese, Thai and lemon basils. Sage, thyme, and rosemary grow in the perennial herb garden next to the Little House, our one-room guest house. The rhubarb and asparagus patches are nearby. A handful of pink stalks is enough for a pie, ten green ones for stir-fry.

During strawberry season – just three weeks in May and June – it takes ten minutes to pick two punnets for shortcake. From June on, there are more squash and cucumbers than we can sell, much less eat, and blueberries are ready on the Fourth of July. In mid-July we pull garlic. Before it dries in the barn, 'wet' garlic is mild and sweet, a special treat.

When the tomatoes come in, summer is in full swing. We grow some two dozen different varieties in red, yellow, orange, purple, pink, and green. There are dense plum tomatoes, heavy beefsteaks, tiny cherry tomatoes, and funny-looking heritage varieties.

The farm is at its best on Friday nights, when we load six or seven trucks for four Saturday markets. The basement, the converted greenhouse, the shady place under the trees, and the barn are overflowing with freshly picked produce. There are red, yellow, and orange bell peppers; yellow, purple, and green french beans; cantaloupes and watermelons; mustard and rape greens; tomatoes and aubergines; and various smaller crops – chillies, okra, basil, beets, chard, garlic, raspberries. A master chart shows what goes to which market. *Arlington*, it might say: *29 half bushels of tomatoes: 13 Lady Lucks, 5 Pink Girls, 5 Lemon Boys, 2 Brandywines, 4 Pineapples*. From the kitchen, I can hear the trucks being loaded and people calling out what goes where. By nine o'clock, the trucks are lined up in the driveway, ready for market. They leave at five in the morning.

Farming is hard work, but when we sit down to dinner we feel lucky. When everyone has had a bath, I set the table on the porch and open a bottle of Gamay from our friends' vineyard across the way. We start with a plate of sliced tomatoes or a bowl of salsa. There are always two or three vegetables, and dessert is fruit pie. The moon rises over the pond and the crickets chirp. It is still warm at eleven o'clock. My mother sighs – her way of saying, *This is luxury*. We all think so.

THE
FARMERS'
MARKET

In London I found myself homesick, not for the farm where I grew up, but for fresh, seasonal produce. My garden was tiny. I didn't have a car to drive to pick-your-own places and farm shops. I had tried organic box schemes: they were expensive, and too often the produce was the worse for wear and imported. I didn't want to eat Israeli tomatoes in January, even if they were organic – they had travelled too far and didn't taste good. Even when my delivery contained British produce, it came from the middle-man, not the farmer.

I knew what I wanted. I wanted fresh English food in season, straight from the farm. I wanted to learn from farmers about the growing season and good varieties. I wanted ripe tomatoes in August, traditional apples, local asparagus, fresh sweetcorn, and delicious strawberries. I decided to start a weekly farmers' market, exclusively for farmers selling home-grown produce.

I rented a site and set about finding farmers. It was slow going. No one knew about farmers' markets. 'Our members wouldn't be interested,' said the National Farmers Union. With falling farm prices and income, this seemed a blinkered view. (Today the NFU supports farmers' markets.) Eventually I found producers selling fruit and vegetables, pork, chicken, goat's cheese, eggs, honey, breads, flowers, herbs, wines, and juice. All the farms were within a hundred miles of the market, many closer. Some were organic.

The Islington Farmers' Market was the first in London. When Agriculture Minister Nick Brown rang the opening bell on Sunday, 6 June 1999, people were fighting to get to the salad leaves. They were like locusts. In four hours, nothing was left. I bought the last carrot. Three months later I opened two more weekly markets, in Notting Hill and Swiss Cottage, and within six months I had quit my job at the American embassy to start farmers' markets full-time. In 2000 we organised seven weekly markets in London. Markets were appearing all over the country. In 2000 Britain had some 250 farmers' markets.

In one sense, farmers' markets are not new. Farmers have been selling produce in market towns since Roman days. Only a generation ago, local market gardeners supplied London greengrocers. We ate strawberries at Wimbledon and russets in October. But global agriculture trade changed all that. Now supermarkets sell everything, all year round. Farmers' markets restore something lost, but not forgotten – contact with the seasons.

WHAT IS FOR SALE AT THE FARMERS' MARKET?

The farmers' market is at once a greengrocer, butcher, baker, deli, florist, garden centre, and fishmonger. Along with fruit, vegetables, and salads, farmers sell lamb, beef, pork, chicken, venison, cheese, eggs, honey, wine, juice, mushrooms, jams, jellies, chutneys, baked goods, plants, cut flowers, and herbs. There are homemade meat pies, quiches, smoked chicken and fish, flavoured sausages and pâtés.

There are native foods like watercress, as well as locally grown imports, like fennel and wild rocket. There are traditional, or heritage, varieties of fruits and vegetables and the meat of rare-breed animals. There are unusual things, like striped beetroots, golden courgettes, giant ostrich eggs, unfiltered honey, and bee pollen.

There are wild-caught foods, including game, mussels, lobster, and crab. Farmers gather sloes for gin, damsons, blackberries, mushrooms, and elderflowers from the wild. In December they sell Christmas puddings, bronze turkeys, geese, goose dripping, mistletoe, and Christmas trees.

If you don't know what it is or how to cook it, just ask. The lamb lady sells rosemary and gives out recipes. The bee-keeper brings bees to market and explains why raw local honey is good for allergies. You may learn how to use wild garlic, what free-range means, or the difference between a green and a red pepper. (The red one is ripe.)

HOW GREEN IS MODERN AGRICULTURE?

Most commercial growers routinely use toxic chemicals. Unacceptable levels of organophosphates, DDT, and other chemicals, some of them illegal in the UK, have been found on supermarket produce. The average lettuce receives eleven pesticide treatments; 99 per cent of eating pears are treated with fungicides, 91 per cent with growth promoters. Nitrogen and phosphorus run-off from overuse of fertilisers pollutes rivers and harms wildlife.

Driven to get higher yields at lower cost, meat, dairy, and egg producers use ever more antibiotics, growth promoters, and hormones. They use low-quality, cheap feed – such as scrapie-infected sheep brains, which led to the BSE crisis. Animals suffer from overcrowding

SWEET PEAS

and lack of room to roam. The result is high infection and disease rates, which are then treated with more chemicals. On fish farms, dirty water and small pens cause sea lice infestation, which is doused with pesticides. These practices do nothing for the flavour and quality of the food.

The apologists for chemically intensive agriculture say they merely want to produce cheaper food for the public. But the public pays the final bill. The prices farmers receive are declining and the consumer gets low-quality food. Human health and the environment suffer.

Many farmers reject these chemically intensive methods as harmful and counterproductive. They employ various alternatives, some traditional, others cutting-edge. Instead of using chemical fertilisers, they build soil fertility with leguminous crops and composted animal manure. Instead of pesticides that harm songbirds and damage human health, they use row covers, companion planting, and beneficial insects. Instead of fumigants to kill soil-borne diseases, they use crop rotation. Instead of herbicides that reduce biodiversity, they keep weeds down by mechanical means and mulch. Instead of dosing animals with antibiotics, they use homeopathic remedies and allow animals more room, so disease is less likely to spread.

These methods protect humans and the environment from poisonous chemicals. Another reason to farm green is nutritional. A small but growing set of data suggests that produce grown in chemical-free, sustainable ways is nutritionally superior, with more vitamins, minerals, trace elements, protein, and anti-oxidants.

13

Of all the farmers using these green methods, organic farmers are the best known. They can be certified by an authority such as the Soil Association, which conducts regular inspections to ensure organic methods are used. Biodynamic growing pre-dates organic farming and is sometimes referred to as organic-plus. Biodynamic farmers use organic methods as well as special planting calendars and crop rotations to improve yields and nutritional value. Demeter is the biodynamic certification authority. Any farmer at the market claiming to be organic or biodynamic should display the appropriate certificate.

Many farmers at farmers' markets use some or all of these methods, but their produce does not fit any of the established labels. On these farms, the apples are unsprayed, the lamb is additive-free, the chickens roam freely on untreated pasture. Before organic became a fashionable term and a legal definition, many farmers ran chemical-free, natural farms. Many still do.

On our farm, we always grew most crops without herbicides, insecticides, and fungicides. Now we use none at all. We have always fed our soil and plants with composted manure, leguminous crops, and a sea water-based nutritional supplement rich in trace elements. We mulch and hand-weed to control weeds and use natural remedies for the few pests we have. The sea water solution cannot be certified organic. It is, however, healthy for plants, people and the planet. Our soil is rich and crumbly, our plants thrive, and our fruit and vegetables taste great.

Only certified farms may label their produce 'organic' or 'biodynamic'. But the wise green consumer should look beyond the label for healthy food and farming methods. At the market you can develop a rapport with the farmers. They should want to earn your trust, and to win your business, they will respond to your requests.

WHICH TOMATO? GROWN WHERE?

Does organic food taste better? Sometimes. The three most important factors for flavour are proper maturity and ripeness, freshness, and a good-tasting variety. Much imported organic fruit is grown for the same shipping qualities as other mass-produced fruit: it is hard, thick-skinned, and tolerates mechanical harvesting. Even organic produce can be picked green, stored too long, and ripened artificially. The farm may not pollute the rivers, but the tomatoes are tasteless. Farmers who care about taste grow varieties with superior flavour, pick them at the right time, and sell them fresh. When I hear someone say, 'We buy organic tomatoes because they taste better,' I always think, Which tomato? Grown where?

WHAT IS BIODIVERSITY?

Biodiversity can refer to many species living in one eco-system, or multiple varieties of one plant or animal. Biodiversity increases food security and preserves valuable traits. Chemically intensive farming favours mono-cropping, but single crops are more vulnerable to frost, pests, or disease. The Irish potato famine is a famous example. Over-reliance on one variety can also reduce biodiversity further down the line. Cox apples, for example, are particularly vulnerable to pests, so farmers use more insecticides, which kill beneficial insects and reduce the food supply of songbirds. It is a downward spiral: fewer apple varieties, fewer insects, fewer songbirds.

When varieties are lost, valuable traits are lost too. Sturmer apples contain 20 milligrams Vitamin C per 100 grams, five times greater than Golden Delicious with 4 milligrams. But few people know Sturmers, because 70 per cent of the eating apples in the UK are Cox and Bramley. Rare-breed animals, many of which are near extinction, often have better flavour, and can be hardier than their intensively bred cousins. The British Saddleback pig, for example, grazes better.

Why is there more variety at farmers' markets? Farmers selling directly to the consumer seek different qualities from the big growers, distributors, and retailers, so they grow forgotten varieties and breeds. They want nice texture, for example, rather than shelf-life, nutritional value rather than heavy cropping, flavoursome meat rather than docile animals. Growing and rearing different varieties and breeds is fun, too. Who wants to plant, pick, sell, and eat the same plum for twenty years?

EAT FOODS IN PEAK SEASON

Produce tastes best when it is in season and locally grown – exactly what the farmers' market offers. At the market there are no strawberries in January. But techniques such as poly-tunnels, long-season varieties and improved storage conditions have stretched even local growing seasons. For the very best flavour, eat produce at peak season – the plant's natural peak, when it is cropping heavily outdoors.

Why buy in peak season? A common side effect of breeding plants for extended seasons is loss of other qualities, such as flavour. Peak season produce is more likely to be of a traditional variety, with outstanding flavour or texture. Peak season produce is less likely to have been stored a long time, losing nutrients and flavour. Stored produce is often treated with waxes, preservatives, and fungicides.

Produce in peak season is more likely to be grown outdoors in real soil, rather than under glass, in sterile soil substitutes (substrate), or in a water bath with liquid fertilisers (hydroponically). English cucumbers and courgettes in May, for example, must be grown under glass. Fruit and vegetables grown in open sun and soil taste better and are more nutritious. Soil minerals, which vary from farm to farm, impart specific flavours and nutrients. This is the French *terroir*, the idea that the distinctive features of a small piece of land – soil type, moisture, frost, wind patterns – impart special character to the grapes and thus the wine. *Terroir* is even at work in cheese and meat. Have you ever wondered why all supermarket vegetables taste alike, or why the potted herbs in substrate are insipid and die in three days? They have no *terroir*.

One season-extending technology widely used by farmers, including 'green' farmers, is the poly-tunnel. A piece of plastic stretched over the plants like a gardener's cloche, it traps the sun and warms the soil, which adds a few extra weeks at the beginning and end of the season.

The season for strawberries, asparagus, and rhubarb is often extended with poly-tunnels. Mediterranean crops like tomatoes, aubergines, and peppers often need poly-tunnels all summer in our climate. If they are good varieties grown in healthy soil, they should be tasty.

GROWING IT ALL BACK HOME: A Complete Revolution in British Cookery

Cookery writers try to define native cooking, but it is an elusive concept. Like culture, food is never static, but constantly subject to new influences. In the 1950s, Elizabeth David introduced Mediterranean flavours to Britain. Now olive oil, basil, and garlic are basics in most kitchens. Asian and West Indian immigrants have brought spices into mainstream meals. Curry has long been part of British cookery. With each new ingredient and method, the repertoire of the native cook grows.

Until recently, traditional British cookery was unfashionable. Then food writers like Jane and Sophie Grigson, Henrietta Green, Sybil Kapoor, and Nigel Slater redeemed native dishes and ingredients with style and affection. In her wonderful book *Simply British*, Sybil Kapoor returns to quintessentially British ingredients to define native cooking. Elderflower, oats, haddock, greengages, and lamb remind us of Britain, she says, just as basil, tomatoes, buffalo mozzarella, and rocket suggest Italy.

The British palate has come to appreciate many new vegetables, from fennel to cavolo nero to rocket. But for a long time such ingredients were imported, expensive, and hard to find. We ate them in smart restaurants or found them in speciality shops. Today these once-exotic crops are grown right here at home. Alongside native damsons, Egremont Russets, and watercress at the farmers' market are many ingredients one may still think of as foreign: fennel, fresh buffalo cheese, rocket, chillies, basil, cavolo nero.

With the spread of farmers' markets, the cooking revolution has moved from the cookbook and the kitchen to the countryside. For introducing us to new ingredients, we must thank the cookery writers and chefs. For growing these crops and bringing them to market, we are indebted to farmers all over Britain.

For a list of London farmers' markets see www.londonfarmersmarkets.com,
email info@lfm.demon.co.uk, or send a stamped addressed envelope to: 6 St Paul Street, London N1 7AB.

For a complete list of farmers' markets in Britain, see www.farmersmarkets.net
or send a SAE to: National Association of Farmers' Markets, South Vaults,
Green Park Station, Green Park Road, Bath BA1 1JS.

HOW TO USE THIS BOOK

Fruit and vegetables are arranged alphabetically, roughly by type and family, but also by how they are used in the kitchen. Pumpkins and winter squash, for example, form one section. They are in the same family and they can be substituted for each other in most recipes. Onions and shallots share a section, but their fellow allium, the leek, has its own.

Each section gives basic information about a fruit or vegetable, including its season, when it is ripe, and how to keep it. 'Making the most of a surplus' tells you what to do when you have more perishable produce than you can eat.

Instead of starting with a recipe, simply buy what looks nice at the farmers' market, supermarket, or wherever you shop for fresh produce. Then read about the fruit or vegetable. Perhaps you will learn a basic recipe (polenta or pizza), discover a new method (smashing garlic), or get an idea (broad bean paste).

As you cook, make substitutions and alter quantities to taste. The recipes are simple and forgiving. They are meant to be eaten at home, not in a restaurant. No recipe is immutable, anyway: it is merely a record of a meal someone somewhere enjoyed once. I think healthy eating is important, but the recipes are not low-fat. Nor are they rich. They suit me, but if your tastes lean in either direction, adjust them.

My cooking philosophy is best expressed in the recipes, but here are some maxims.

Ignore fashion. If you don't like balsamic vinegar, don't use it.

Forget what's 'authentic'. I used to run out of stock when making risotto. Finally I realised that I like it creamy – soft, even – not *al dente*, as it is meant to be. Now I use more stock. You don't serve the recipe. It serves you.

Keep it simple. Let one ingredient star, or stick to unbeatable pairings like tomato and basil.

Be inventive. I adore our family recipe for cucumber salad. I have chopped it up to make salsa (though it is not Mexican) and puréed it for gazpacho (though it is not Spanish).

I hope the book makes you a more adventurous, confident, and independent cook. If you were to buy Jerusalem artichokes at the farmers' market, read about them here, try one recipe, tweak it to suit, discover you love Jerusalem artichokes, and never use a recipe again, this book would be a success. Cooking without lists, without recipes, without scales and measures, is one of life's great pleasures. Eating food the way you like it is another. Please yourself.

SERVINGS

On the assumption that many of us cook regularly for a few people, many recipes serve two or four. 'Serves 2 to 4' means the recipe makes two servings if it is the only vegetable you are eating, or four if you are eating other vegetables.

Parsley means the flat-leafed kind. *Sugar* is caster sugar. Some recipes call for vanilla pods, which are lovely, but not cheap. One teaspoon of real vanilla extract is usually a good substitute. *Vanilla sugar* makes the pod go further. Split a pod and keep it in a jar of sugar. It keeps for months. *Cayenne, Serrano*, or *Jalapeño* peppers will usually do for fresh chilli, but if the variety of pepper matters it is specified. *Pepper* means freshly ground black peppercorns. *Mustard seed*, yellow or brown, is a wonderful spice, cheap and easy to find.

Salt means any sea salt, rich in trace elements and iodine, an essential nutrient. If it matters whether you use flakes or rock salt, the recipe says so.

A word about salt in cooking. Sodium is an essential nutrient, but processed foods contain far too much – an attempt to compensate for lack of flavour and freshness. But fresh, whole foods need salt, too. Starchy vegetables and grains don't taste right if they are not salted during cooking. Salt enhances flavour, even making sweet things taste sweeter. Mind the salt in stocks, especially store-bought, or you will over-salt the final dish.

Buy locally produced untreated *honey*. Commercial honey is filtered, blended, and cooked. This process destroys flavour, as well as trace elements and pollen, which can relieve allergies. Raw honey has the distinctive taste of local, seasonal flowers. Gardeners rely on bees for pollination – another reason to buy local honey.

Best olive oil means the best you can afford. Use it cold, when the taste really matters – say, for crostini and special dressings. *Olive oil* is for everyday use – good-quality oil for dressings, marinades and sautéing. For health and flavour, olive and other vegetable oils must be cold-pressed, extra-virgin. Cook them as little as possible.

Oil for frying means a basic vegetable oil such as 'light' olive (less flavour but not less fat), when you don't want the flavour of olive oil. It will not be extra-virgin. Store oils in a cool, dark place and use them quickly.

Some processed foods are cheap, nutritious, tasty, and just what a busy cook needs. Tinned tomatoes (whole and Passata, see p. 215) are essential. Dried chick peas and cannellini beans take hours to cook; I use tinned. To deepen their flavour, cook them in their stock with sautéed garlic or herbs. I do make my own stock (see p. 219), but store-bought is handy. I use an organic one, Kallo, in many flavours.

Most importantly, a note on the main ingredients – fruit and vegetables. Variety names such as *Opal* (a courgette) are in italics. I hope this encourages cooks to seek out superior varieties, and farmers to grow them.

There are some seven thousand apple varieties, but only about a hundred are grown commercially. Britain is ideal apple country. Sadly, more than 60 per cent of its apple orchards have vanished since 1970. Just two varieties – *Cox* and *Bramley* – account for 70 per cent of the apples we eat in Britain. Instead of stocking other native varieties, the supermarkets are overflowing with New Zealand *Galas*, French *Braeburns* and American *Red Delicious*.

At the farmers' market there are English *Braeburns*, *Galas,* and *Red Delicious*, not to mention *Discovery, Worcester Pearmain, Blenheim Orange, Laxton Superb, Jupiter, Spartan, Winston*. Some farmers grow more than a hundred varieties. One of the best reasons to buy local produce is learning about forgotten fruit.

The way to learn apple season is by eating them, but a rough guide helps. *Discovery* arrive first, as early as August. In late August and September, *Katy, Worcester Pearmain, Greensleeves,* and *James Grieve* arrive. *Spartan, Cox's Orange Pippin,* and *Egremont Russet* come in late September and October.

Farmers bring selected apples from controlled-atmosphere storage through winter and spring. *Crowngolds* and *Jonagoreds*, two red-yellow large, juicy eating apples, may be crisp in May. *Ida Red* and *Red Pippin* are good keepers. In general, a smaller apple stores better.

Unlike pears, which must be picked underripe, apples should ripen on the tree. Supermarket *Russets* are seldom ripe. The skin and flesh are greenish. They taste sharp, not nutty.

Cooking apples are tart, acidic, and collapse like cotton wool when cooked. *Bramley* is the classic. *Howgate Wonder* and *Lord Derby* are others. *Blenheim Orange* is a 'sweet cooker'. Dessert or eating apples are sweeter and hold their shape in tarts and pies. *Winston* are sharp and crisp. Try tasting single-variety juices to learn about flavours.

After giving up using chemicals, organic growers say their fruit is denser with more flavour. Ninety per cent of the organic apples in the UK are imported. If you find organic orchards or those using fewer chemicals, support them.

SEASON

First appear in August, peak in October. Excellent fruit from storage until February. Quality waning by April.

WHAT TO LOOK FOR

No bruises or breaks in the skin. Rough, russeted patches are fine, even desirable. Heavy fruit. Ask if apples have been sprayed, when, and how often.

STORAGE

A cool place, not the fridge, for several weeks in peak season, less in the spring. Never with other vegetables. The ethylene released by apples causes green vegetables to spoil faster and makes carrots bitter.

MAKING THE MOST OF A SURPLUS

Apple sauce is easy to make and keeps well.

CHARLOTTE'S EASY BRAMLEY SPONGE CAKE WITH CUSTARD

*'**Bramley** – still the best for cooking.' So reads the sign at the Deme's stall on the farmers' markets. Charlotte Deme helps sell the fruit grown on her family's orchard in Chegworth Valley, Kent. The acidic yoghurt helps the sponge rise. Use a baking tin about 35 x 25 cm.*

*   * **Bramleys** are sour; if you want the apple layer less tangy, sprinkle them with sugar. Or use a sweeter, eating apple, like **Jonagored** or **Cox's Orange Pippin**.*

SERVES 8–10

800 g *Bramleys* (5–6 medium)

200 g unsalted butter, softened

150 g Vanilla Sugar (see p. 19)

4 large eggs

1/4 tsp real vanilla extract

3 tbsp yoghurt

2 tsp baking powder

200 g flour

- Set the oven to 160°C and put in the tin to warm.
- Peel the apples. Hold each apple upright on its stem end, and cut thin slices downward on four sides. The slices will be round, then square.
- Butter the tin and layer the apples in it.
- Cream the butter and sugar, then add the eggs, yoghurt, and vanilla extract, mixing well.
- Mix the dry ingredients well. Fold quickly into the butter mixture. When the batter is evenly mixed, spread it over the apples, right to the edge of the pan, and smooth the top. The apples will shrink and the sponge rise, so do not worry about the exact fit.
- Bake for 35–40 minutes or until a cocktail stick stuck in the middle comes out clean. Serve warm with Custard (see p 218).

APPLE SAUCE

*Again, if you use a sharp cooking apple such as **Bramley** or **Lord Derby**, you may need some honey, but not with eating apples like **Crowngold** or **Jonagored**.*

SERVES 4

6 large sweet eating apples, peeled, cored and diced

1/4 tsp cinnamon

sprinkle of salt (optional)

- Cook the apples with the cinnamon until they are soft. Mash or run them through a mouli until smooth. A sprinkle of salt may bring out the flavour.

TARTE TATIN

Even the home cook needs the odd spectacular displays, and Tarte Tatin, after the eponymous Tatin sisters, or tarte renversée, *is one. Apples, pears, or peaches are caramelised in a frying-pan, pastry goes on top, and when it's baked you turn it upside down to reveal the sugary fruit, with the crust on the bottom.*

No apologies for the way I finally made Tarte Tatin foolproof: I use a small pan, which gives you more control over the crucial flipping bit. The frying-pan must be ovenproof and should be heavy. The more apples you can cram in, the better. They shrink.

SERVES 6–8

4–6 *Cox's Orange Pippins*

juice of 1 lemon

3 tbsp sugar

large knob butter

½ quantity Shortcrust Pastry (see p 218)

- Peel, halve and core apples. Leave one half whole, and quarter the others. Toss in the lemon juice to stop them oxidising (going brown).
- In the frying-pan, caramelise the sugar by heating it gently until it bubbles and browns. When it turns dark, add the butter and mix well.
- Set the oven to 180°C.
- Pack the apples in the frying-pan, round side down (they will be showing later), as close together as possible. Put the half apple in the centre and cover.
- Cook gently until the apples are half soft and the syrup is reduced a bit. Remove from the heat and cool.
- Roll out the pastry. When the pan is cool, lay the pastry over it, tucking it down between the apples and the sides of the pan. This makes a little wall to hold in the apples and juice when the tart is flipped.
- Bake for 25–30 minutes, until the crust is golden brown, and cool slightly.
- Now for the moment of truth: cover the pan with a large, flat serving dish. Using oven gloves, hold the pan underneath with your strong hand, and keep the plate in place with your weak hand. In one swift, controlled motion, turn the pan over and set the dish down. Keep the plate and the pan in place as if you were holding something precious between them – you are. Gently jiggle the pan to release the pastry and sticky apples. Survey your masterpiece and serve warm with ice cream.

Variation: Use peaches, plums or pears. Try peaches unpeeled more flavour. Use Vanilla Sugar (see p 19), or grate fresh nutmeg over the pears.

NORA'S ROAST PORK CHOPS WITH APPLE & HORSERADISH STUFFING

*Washington, DC's smarter restaurants used to be steak houses or high Italian. In 1979 Nora Pouillon opened **Restaurant Nora**, serving additive-free, seasonal produce with Mediterranean flavours, buying from local organic farms wherever possible. In 1999 Nora's became America's first certified organic restaurant. Just round the corner is Dupont Circle farmers' market, handy for heritage tomatoes from the Plancks' stall.*

SERVES 4

2 tbsp oil for frying

1 large eating apple, grated

1 large shallot, finely chopped

4-cm piece horseradish, about 4 tbsp grated

1 tbsp Dijon mustard

salt and pepper

4 pork chops, about 4 cm thick

For the glaze

6 tbsp balsamic vinegar

3 tbsp honey

- Set the oven to 180ºC.
- Sauté the apple and shallot in 2 tablespoons of the oil for 2–4 minutes all until soft. Remove from the heat add the horseradish, mustard, salt and pepper.
- With a small knife, make a pocket in each pork chop by cutting a 4-cm slice in the side opposite the bone, parallel with the two faces of the chop. Move the knife in an arc, back and forth, cutting a large interior pocket in the meat but keeping the opening small.
- Push as much apple stuffing into the pocket as you can. The chop will be plump and rounded.
- To make the glaze, gently simmer the vinegar and honey until it is reduced by about one-third.
- Brush the chops with half of the glaze, sprinkle with salt and pepper, and put them in the oven.
- After about 15 minutes, brush the chops with more glaze.
- Roast for about 30 minutes total, or until the chops and stuffing are cooked through. Serve with Braised Red Cabbage (see p. 69).

Variation: Stuff with Braised Red Cabbage (see p. 69), grating instead of slicing the apples.

ASIAN
GREENS

Cool-weather-loving Asian greens are a perfect year-round green vegetable at the farmers' market. Asian vegetables are members of the sharp-tasting *brassica* (broccoli) family. They come in purple, red, pale green to almost black, frilly or flat, round or ruffled, and in all sizes.

We can divide Asian vegetables unscientifically by looks. The first sort are cabbage-like. They have green leaves on juicy, crunchy white stems and stalks, and they include Chinese cabbage (*Ruffles*), misome, and several pak chois. Chinese cabbage is cylindrical and pale green. It can be squat or taller, with a big white rib. *Santoh* is a non-heading Chinese cabbage, with large, pale green leaves. Misome, tat tsai, and pak choi *Joi Choi* are rosette pak chois, which make a little flower-like cluster of dark, shiny leaves on juicy white stems. Some farmers sell baby tat tsai and pak choi leaves. They are nice in salads, but neither tastier nor more tender than larger ones.

The second kind are smaller and leafier, without the succulent white stem. They taste of mustard, from mild to sharp. They include mizuna and mibuna, which look a bit like rocket, with thin, often feathery leaves. There are many mustards, such as the flat *Green in Snow*, frilly *Green Wave*, and the veiny, grooved *Red Giant*. *Komatsuna* is a milder mustard. *Hon Tsai Tai* (red stems) and *Autumn Poem* (all green) have a sweet, mild mustard flavour.

In the kitchen both kinds of Asian vegetables work equally well in stir-fries, soups, and salads. The cabbage-like kind are milder. Use the tender, thick white stems raw in salads as well as the leaves, or steam them briefly.

In salads, the mustards are best used as an accent to a milder lettuce. Mustard leaves – even large ones – are wonderful steamed with olive oil and vinegar. Do not overcook them. Wilted with olive oil, mizuna and mibuna are a nice accent on pasta – almost like an herb, there is so little leaf.

Other Asian vegetables are Chinese kale (*Green Lance*) and *Choy Sum Purple Flowering*, which are something like purple-sprouting broccoli, with tender stems and flowerheads. Japanese parsley tastes like a parsley-celery cross.

SEASON

Asian greens are available all year, depending on the variety, farmer, and weather.

WHAT TO LOOK FOR

Perky, turgid, shiny leaves, no bruises, creases, or yellowing. Stems should be pure white, no brown spots.

STORAGE

Like lettuce, in a plastic bag with some air in it in the fridge. Use in 2–4 days. The cabbage-like ones last a week.

MAKING THE MOST OF A SURPLUS

Soups and stir-fries. Asian greens cook down fast. A large volume of raw greens makes only a small serving cooked.

PAD THAI

*Make the spice paste and chop everything before you start cooking. Soak the noodles just as you begin to sauté. When you've made all the preparations, it should take about 15 minutes to cook. Look for fish sauce, often called **Nuoc nam**, in Vietnamese shops. It's a strong, salty stock usually made with anchovies. Tamarind is a dense brown paste.*

SERVES 4

500 g rice noodles

2–3 tbsp olive oil (or cold-pressed sesame)

16–20 prawns

about 500 g green vegetables, chopped (pak choi, tat soi, mizuna, Chinese cabbage, beansprouts, broccoli, mangetout)

2 tbsp soy sauce

1 fresh chilli pepper, finely chopped (optional)

2 tbsp fresh coriander, chopped

2 tbsp peanuts, crushed

For the spice paste

1 tbsp fresh lime juice

3 tbsp fish sauce

2 tbsp tamarind, mixed with water or fish sauce

2 tbsp sugar

2 fresh chillies, finely chopped

2 shallots, finely chopped

- Make the spice paste by pounding together all the ingredients in a mortar and pestle or chopping briefly in a food-processor.
- Bring to the boil enough salted water to cover the noodles. Add the noodles, turn off the heat, and leave to soak. When they have rehydrated, drain them, reserving some of the water.
- Heat the oil with the spice paste in a large sauté pan or wok, with room for the vegetables and noodles. Sauté the prawns until they are bright pink, about 2 minutes.
- Add the vegetables, coat them with the oil and sauté until tender. (Broccoli will take longer than the others, so cut the pieces small or add them first.)
- Put in the noodles, soy sauce, some chilli to taste, and black pepper. Mix well until noodles are heated through. If it's a bit dry, moisten with noodle water. Top with chopped coriander, the rest of the chillies, and the peanuts.

SPICY SALAD

SERVES 4

2 large handfuls mixed spicy greens,
  such as red or green mustard,
  mizuna, mibuna, or misome
1 large head leaf lettuce, such as oak leaf
1 small turnip, grated
1 small radish, chopped fine

For the dressing
3 tbsp + 1 tsp best olive oil
1 tbsp apple or pear juice
1 clove garlic, smashed, peeled, and
  finely chopped

- Put the dressing ingredients into a small jar and shake well. Season.
- Remove the stems from the greens and tear the lettuce into bite-sized pieces. Add the turnip and radish. Toss well with dressing and salt.

RAINBOW TROUT
WITH ASIAN GREENS

This is almost soup. Eat Japanese rice on the side, or in the stock.

SERVES 2

1 tbsp sesame seeds

100 g Asian greens such as pak choi,
tat soi, mizuna, misome, mibuna,
mitsuba, Chinese mustard
(*Green Wave* or *Green in Snow*,
Red Giant)

400 g delicate vegetables in season,
such as peas (shelled or mangetout,
yellow summer squash, french beans,
baby carrots)

2 large cloves garlic, smashed, peeled,
and finely chopped

2-cm chunk ginger, peeled in ribbons with
a vegetable peeler

1 fresh red chilli, sliced in rounds if mild,
finely chopped if hot (or to taste)

2 tbsp sesame oil

2 tbsp fish sauce (see Pad Thai, p. 28)
or light soy sauce

500 ml water

2 fresh rainbow trout fillets

2 spring onions, diced

- Toast the sesame seeds in a dry frying-pan until they are light brown. Do not let them burn. Remove them from the pan and set them aside.
- Do all the chopping. If the Asian greens are very small, leave them whole. Pak choi stems, mangetout and other vegetables should be bite-sized.
- Sauté the garlic, ginger, and half of the chilli in the sesame oil. Add the fish sauce and water and simmer to reduce a bit. Put in the fish and poach it for about 5 minutes. Remove it from the pan and keep it warm.
- Add the vegetables and half of the spring onions and cook until crisp-tender. Check seasoning.
- Set each fish in a large, flat serving bowl, and cover with stock. Top with chillies, spring onions, sesame seeds and a little sesame oil.

ASPARAGUS

Forget whether the stalks are thick or thin. All that matters is that they are mature and fresh.

To see whether asparagus is fresh, look at the bottom. Every day the white scab on the cut end gets harder. The spear should be crispy, not rubbery. Farmers should store asparagus in a cool shady place in buckets of cold water or wrapped in moist cloth.

Judging maturity takes more training. It helps to understand how farmers grow and pick asparagus. Asparagus is expensive because the stalks must be harvested one by one. They also grow fast and have to be picked every day. One day, the shoot is 15 cm high and immature. Twenty-four hours later, it is 22 cm tall and perfect. On the third day, it is 30 cm tall and fibrous. In less than a week, an unchecked spear becomes a 2-metre ferny bush.

The clue to maturity is not size but the little scales on the tip of the stalk. Asparagus is a perennial with ferny branches that grow from the scales. In the spring, the root or crown sends up green spears. Large crowns produce fat stalks, smaller ones thin stalks. When asparagus is too young, the scales are tightly fused. When it is perfect, the scales are short, distinct, and lying flat against the stalk. The tip is smooth. When it is over-mature, the scales are pulling away from the stalk, beginning to send out little branches.

After six or eight weeks, farmers stop picking asparagus to let the spears shoot up and leaf out. The photosynthesising ferny branches feed the crowns, so they can send up next year's crop.

Farmers sometimes blanch asparagus to make it white. Buried under mulch, it is deprived of light and cannot produce chlorophyll. The taste is subtly different. Purple asparagus, another variety, is pretty but, like many purple vegetables, turns green when cooked.

To make the most of it, you must trim asparagus stalk by stalk. **Method 1**: From the cut end, bend the stalk gently; where it snaps is a good place to start. Check the broken stem end. If it is tender, snap further down the stalk. **Method 2**: With a vegetable peeler, peel off the thick skin on the lower end of the stalk. The pale green centre is tender. In any case, save the stem ends. They freeze well, and boiling asparagus ends with a clove of garlic makes a useful stock. The essential rule about asparagus: do not overcook. A couple of minutes in boiling water, lid off, is plenty.

SEASON

In poly-tunnels from early April. The outdoor peak crop is mid- to late April until mid-June.

WHAT TO LOOK FOR

Stiff, bright green stalks with fresh, not scabby, ends; cut not torn. Scales lying flat and close to spear.

STORAGE

Dunk in cold water, pat dry, and wrap it in moist paper or cloth in the fridge. Eat as soon as possible, or within 3 days of purchase.

MAKING THE MOST OF A SURPLUS

It is impossible to buy too much asparagus!

ASPARAGUS WITH
LEMON BASIL VINAIGRETTE

SERVES 2–3

200 g asparagus per person
  (about 250 g untrimmed)
1 quantity Lemon Basil Vinaigrette (see p.189)

- Put the dressing ingredients into a jar, shake well and season. The longer the shallot sits in the oil, the mellower it will be.
- Trim the asparagus and cut it into 5-cm pieces. Bring to the boil in about 3 cm salted water and drop in the asparagus. Cook for 2 minutes, until bright green and crisp-tender.
- Drain and toss with the dressing. Serve warm.

Variation: For a larger green salad, toss 1 large head of mild, sweet-leaf lettuce such as *Embrace* with a bit of olive oil. Sprinkle with salt. Toss in the asparagus with the basil vinaigrette.

RIVER CAFÉ PENNE
WITH ASPARAGUS CARBONARA

*Ruth Rogers and Rose Gray not only search Italian farms and pastures for the best cultivated and wild ingredients. They also grow organic vegetables in the River Café garden. This recipe is from their seasonal cookbook, **Greens**.*

SERVES 2–3

1.5 kg asparagus
400 g penne rigate
8 egg yolks

150 g best Parmesan, freshly grated
100 g butter
3 tbsp thyme leaves, no stalks

- Snap the tough end off each asparagus spear, discard it, and slice the rest diagonally into 2-cm chunks. Keep the tips separate.
- Bring to the boil 2 saucepans of salted water. Start the pasta in one. After a few minutes, blanch the asparagus stalks in the second pan. In 2 minutes, add the tips. In less than 2 more minutes, thin stalks will be crisp-tender; thicker spears may take a minute longer. Remember that asparagus will keep cooking after it is taken off the heat. Drain.
- Beat the egg yolks lightly and season them. Add 2 tablespoons of the Parmesan.
- Melt the butter in a large pan, add the thyme and, soon after, the asparagus. Season and toss.
- Drain the pasta, leaving it a bit moist, and add it to the asparagus. Add the egg yolks and toss. Serve hot with the remaining cheese.

ASPARAGUS WITH SESAME SEEDS

Buy only top-quality cold-pressed sesame oil, refrigerate, and use it quickly. Heat – in pressing, storage, or cooking – makes it go rancid. Cook sesame oil as little as possible.

SERVES 2–4

1 tbsp sesame seeds

1 cm ginger, peeled or finely chopped or
  in ribbons; use a vegetable peeler

1 tbsp + 1 tsp sesame oil

1 bunch asparagus (about 500 g)

- Snap off the ends of the asparagus where the stalk breaks naturally.
- Toast the sesame seeds in a dry frying-pan, shaking constantly until they are golden. Remove.
- In 1 teaspoon of sesame oil, sauté the ginger until it has lost its bite.
- Boil some salted water and drop in the asparagus for 2 minutes or less, depending on its thickness. Drain, and put into the frying-pan with the ginger, sautéing for 1 minute on a high heat.
- Toss with the sesame seeds and the remaining oil. Sprinkle with salt and serve warm.

AUBERGINE

The aubergine is one to eat immature. When over-mature, it is bitter. Unlike other members of the nightshade family (tomatoes and peppers), aubergines do not change colour as they ripen. Small ones are less likely to be over-mature, but these clues work with aubergines of any size: a perfect aubergine is shiny, silky to touch, and gives slightly when squeezed. The green cap is fresh and just a bit loose. An over-mature aubergine is tight and firm like a drum, and the cap strains against the fruit.

At home you will know whether you got it right. Overripe aubergines have big brown seeds, while the seeds of a properly picked aubergine are small and white, and turn brown only when it is cut open. Truly baby aubergines – when the large varieties are picked egg-sized – lack that meaty flavour, and are no more tender than an aubergine properly picked and cooked. The slim Italian and Asian varieties are milder, and the big, egg-shaped violet one holds its shape well for grilling. *Snowy* is tasty and white.

Like all Mediterranean vegetables, aubergines love hot weather, which means they are usually grown in poly-tunnels in Britain. It also means they do not need (or like) very cold storage – a cool pantry at about 10°C is fine. Moisture is lost through their porous skins, but even when an aubergine gets a bit wrinkly, it will still be sweet – it just has less water.

Do not boil or steam aubergine. You want to remove water, not add it. Sauté it in cubes, grill or bake it. Contrary to popular wisdom, there is no need to salt aubergine to remove the bitterness. If it is over-mature, it will be bitter either way. Do not peel it. Aubergines are sponges for oil, so brush it on when grilling, and stir quickly when sautéing – otherwise you will keep pouring it on.

SEASON

July to September (mostly in poly-tunnels).

WHAT TO LOOK FOR

Bright, shiny skin, cap and stem green and fresh. Cap not stretched tightly against flesh. Silky to touch, heavy for its size, gives slightly when pressed.

STORAGE

Like the rest of the nightshade family and most hot-weather vegetables, aubergines should be kept at about 10°C, warmer than the fridge (4–7°C). In a porous or paper bag, lasts 4–5 days.

MAKING THE MOST OF A SURPLUS

Week-old aubergine is delicious; it has only lost water. Cumin Aubergine Dip (p. 38) uses several aubergines easily.

AUBERGINE STEWED WITH GARLIC

SERVES 2–4

1 head garlic, sliced

2 tbsp olive oil

1/2 tsp chilli pepper flakes

3 small aubergines, about 500 g, cut into
    bite-sized cubes

500 ml Passata (see p. 215)

1/4 tsp salt

- In a good-sized heavy pan, sauté the garlic in the oil. For maximum heat, add the chilli flakes at the beginning of cooking. The longer they are in the oil, the hotter the finished dish will be.
- Add the aubergine, Passata, and salt and simmer, covered, until the aubergine is tender but still in cubes.

CUMIN AUBERGINE DIP

SERVES 1–2

2 large aubergines, about 800 g

2 tsp olive oil

1 tbsp yoghurt

large pinch salt

1/4 tsp ground cayenne

1/2 tsp cumin

- Set the oven to 200°C. Prick the aubergines with a fork and bake them until they are completely soft, about 30 minutes.
- When they are cool enough to handle, cut them in half and scoop out the flesh. Let the pulp rest a bit; some juice will come out and without it the dip will be less watery.
- Purée all the ingredients until smooth.

Spin-off: For Parmesan Strips, leave the oven on after you have baked the aubergines. When scooping out the flesh, leave some on the skins and cut them into strips 3-cm wide. Sprinkle with Parmesan, olive oil, and salt, and bake on a lightly oiled sheet until crisp.

RATATOUILLE

A high summer classic in countless versions. The vegetables should be soft, almost creamy, and all melded together. Some people sauté the aubergine first. I like this one-step recipe.

SERVES 6–8

8 cloves garlic, peeled and sliced in slivers

50 g basil leaves washed and torn into strips

1 tbsp fresh thyme, chopped

1 tbsp fresh oregano, chopped

4–5 tbsp olive oil

150 ml Passata (see p. 215)

3/4 tsp salt

3 small or 2 medium aubergines
   (about 500 g), in long strips

3 courgettes, halved and quartered
   lengthways in strips

2 large red or yellow sweet peppers, in strips

6 medium tomatoes, sliced

1 large or 2 medium yellow onions,
   in long thin slices

- Cover the garlic and herbs with the olive oil in a large ceramic baking dish. Don't cook acidic things (like tomatoes) in aluminium.
- Add all of the other ingredients, and mix everything, sloshing it around well. You may need two pans. Deep ones make it soupier. Bake at 180°C for 1½ hours or until the aubergines and courgettes are meltingly tender. Serve hot or cold. Improves the next day.

BEANS

Cooks are familiar with the bean pod at many different stages. We eat baby french or snap beans as haricots verts, with hardly any flesh and undeveloped seeds. A larger, pencil-sized french bean has more flesh, but the seeds are still immature and tender. We allow the seed in runner beans to grow a bit bigger, but still eat the pod. With more mature broad beans, only the seed is edible, the pod is too tough and the flesh has been used up by the growing seed. As the bean ripens further, the seed dries out, its protein value increases, and the skin gets tougher. Eventually it is fully mature: it stores well and will sprout when planted. At this stage, we eat beans as pulses.

Most beans at the farmers' market are french beans (sometimes called dwarf) with juicy flesh. They come green (*Top Crop*), purple (*Royalty*), yellow (*Golden Butter*), and flat (*The Prince*). Purple beans turn green when cooked, but yellow beans (sometimes called wax beans) keep their colour. *Deuil fin Precoce* is green with purple stripes. Sauté french beans or blanch them briefly in salted water until crisp-tender. Do not let them get mushy.

Runner beans have a bigger seed, a tougher but edible pod, and need a bit more cooking. They have a strong flavour, but are tough when over-mature. There are standard and stringless varieties. *Enorma* has a good texture. Broad beans must be shelled and boiled for longer than you think. Later in the season, as the bean gets larger, it is worth peeling off its waxy husk, which is tedious. Best for flavour are *Green Windsor*, which also freezes well, and *Masterpiece Longpod*.

Many beans look alike but taste quite different, so ask for a sample. French beans should be tender, juicy, and sweet. Supermarket varieties are bred for lots of fibre, so they can be picked by machine and have a long shelf life.

SEASON

Broad beans, June and July, getting tough in August. French beans: July to September; up to frost with late varieties. Runner beans: June to September.

WHAT TO LOOK FOR

For french beans, crispness. Break one open: it should snap, not bend, and the seeds should be small.

STORAGE

In a plastic bag in the fridge. Keep dry. Eat in 4–5 days. Do not wash until cooking.

MAKING THE MOST OF A SURPLUS

Tinned and frozen french and runner beans do not have much flavour or texture. When I can be bothered to shell broad beans, I'd rather eat them then and there, but they freeze well. Blanch for 1–2 minutes in plenty of salted water

BROAD BEANS WITH TOASTED ALMONDS

Runner beans also work in this recipe. Cut them in thirds.

SERVES 2–4

500 g broad beans, shelled

3 tbsp whole blanched almonds,
  broken up a bit

1 tbsp best olive oil

lemon basil, chopped

fresh lemon juice

- Boil the beans uncovered in salted water until tender, about 15 minutes. Drain. Don't undercook them: raw beans do not taste nice and are difficult to digest.
- Meanwhile, toast the almonds in a warm frying-pan, until they are brown on both sides. Do not let them burn.
- If you like, remove the bean skins. Toss the beans with the almonds, olive oil, lemon basil, and a squeeze of fresh lemon juice. Sprinkle with salt and serve warm.

BROAD BEAN PASTE

If the broad beans are very young and tender, you may want to skip peeling them after cooking.

SERVES 2–4

500 g broad beans, shelled

1 tbsp fennel leaves, finely chopped
  (a bit of white stalk is okay)

4 tbsp best olive oil

2 tbsp fresh lemon juice

$1/4$ tsp salt, or to taste

black pepper to taste

- Boil the beans in salted water with the lid off until tender, about 15 minutes. Drain, reserving some of the cooking water. Cool slightly, and remove the skins if you want to.
- Purée thoroughly with fennel, oil, lemon juice, salt, and pepper. Add 2–3 tablespoons of the cooking water to thin, and check the seasoning.
- Spread on toasted bread or eat on slices of vegetable such as fennel.

MINESTRONE

Minestrone is a soup for all seasons and all sorts of vegetables, but the only essential summer ingredient, to my mind, is french beans (round or flat). Minestrone needs one other green vegetable – spinach, courgettes, asparagus, broad beans, peas – a pulse, and pasta. With the minimum ingredients, minestrone's ready in 20 minutes. This version takes about 40.

SERVES 4–6

2 yellow onions, chopped

4 large cloves garlic, crushed, peeled,
  and chopped

2 bay leaves

1/4 tsp chilli pepper flakes

3 tbsp parsley, finely chopped

4–6 tbsp olive oil, to taste

200 g *Chestnut* cap mushrooms, sliced

3 x 400-g tins tomatoes, chopped

2 x 400-g tins chick peas, cannellini or
  borlotti beans

2 spring onions, chopped

250 g green beans, round or flat,
  in 3-cm slices

1/2 tsp salt

250 g short pasta

2 large handfuls of greens such as
  Swiss chard or spinach, chopped

black pepper

best olive oil to garnish

freshly grated good Parmesan

- Sauté onions, garlic, bay leaves, chilli flakes, and half of the parsley in the olive oil. When soft, add the mushrooms for 2–3 minutes.
- Bring a saucepan of salted water to the boil for the pasta.
- Add the tomatoes, tinned pulses with their juice, spring onions, and beans. Stir well, salt, and simmer.
- In another pan, cook pasta until slightly under-done, 7–8 minutes. Drain, saving the water, and keep warm.
- Add the greens to the soup and simmer until the vegetables are just soft. Don't overcook them. With 5 minutes to go, add the pasta. Add salt, pepper, and more chilli to taste.
- The soup can sit for a few hours if you like the pasta tomato-soaked. It will thicken – just reheat it and thin with a little of the reserved pasta water.
- Top with the remaining parsley, a bit of olive oil, and cheese. Eat with thick bread.

PETER GORDON'S BROAD BEAN & PANCETTA SALAD

*From lime leaves to lemon grass, coriander to cayenne, Peter Gordon brought Asian flavours from New Zealand to his London restaurant, the **Sugar Club**. This ever-so-English vegetable with chilli and tahini is from **Cook at Home with Peter Gordon**. Stuff it in pitta bread or eat as a side dish. It's nice warm.*

SERVES 2–4

300 g broad beans, shelled

2 tbsp olive oil

50 g pancetta, diced, or a palm-sized
  piece of smoked bacon

medium onion, finely sliced

fresh chilli, finely chopped, with seeds
  and pith if you like it hot

2 cloves garlic, smashed, peeled, and
  finely chopped

1 tbsp tahini

1 tbsp balsamic vinegar

1 tbsp mint, chopped

4 pitta breads

crème fraîche (optional)

- Cook the broad beans until tender, about 15 minutes depending on their size. Drain. When they are cool, slip them from their skins.
- Heat the oil in a large frying-pan and fry the pancetta gently until browned. Add the onion and chilli and stir until soft.
- Add garlic and sauté gently until soft but not brown. Finally, add broad beans, mix together, and remove from heat.
- Mix the tahini, vinegar, and mint and toss with the beans. Check the seasoning.
- Stuff into the pitta breads with a dollop of crème fraîche.

BEETROOT &
SWISS CHARD

Beet greens and Swiss chard are some of the dark leafy greens the nutritionists keep badgering you to eat. The wonderful beetroot has much to offer. With an astonishing 8 per cent sugar by weight, it is hardly a bitter pill for all the vitamin C and beta-carotene it contains. It is both sweet and savoury. You eat both the green tops and the root warm or cold. It is a spring, summer, and winter vegetable. First come the delicate, velvety greens. When they are small, put them into salads. Later, steam them like spinach. Then, in June, the small, tender, sweet root arrives. Eat it whole, roasted or steamed. By autumn the root is meatier and more flavourful. Beetroot is delicious raw, grated with apple in a winter salad. Not least, beetroot is a superb winter keeper, at the farm or at home.

They come in all colours. There are white beetroots (*Albino, Blankoma*). *Burpees Golden* is the famous orange beetroot. *Chioggia* is a traditional Italian variety with vivid pink and white stripes; also called candy beetroot, it cooks a bit faster, and doesn't bleed fuchsia juice all over the plate. *Cylindra* is long and tubular rather than round, so it makes even slices. *Regala Baby Beetroot* is tender and sweet, small even when mature.

Do not peel beetroot, unless it is rough around the shoulders, where the stems are. If you must peel it, at least cook it with the skin on to save nutrients. For a quick salad, grate beetroot and apple and dress with olive oil. For a quick version of pickled beetroot, add dill and thin onion slices to cooked beetroot. Drench in the marinade for My Grandmother's Cucumber Salad (see page 88), and leave overnight.

Swiss chard is a member of the same family, but lacks a tasty root. It has large, dark green leaves, wide flat stems with a slightly milder flavour than beetroot. *Silverado* has white stems and a delicate flavour. Rhubarb chard (*Vulcan*) is ruby-coloured, and rainbow chard (*Bright Lights*) has lovely pink, orange, and yellow stems. Very young leaves can be eaten in salads, but chard is best cooked. Chop the stems and leaves separately, and cook the stems first, until they are tender and sweet. Chard is good in soups and stir-fries, or steamed like spinach.

SEASON

Beet greens: from May. Little beetroot: from June; larger beetroot: through November. Often a second crop of new beetroot in late summer. Stored beetroot all winter. Swiss chard: May to November.

WHAT TO LOOK FOR

Fresh green leaves and unblemished roots. The taproot should not be dried out. Heavy for their size, and not wrinkly. White-grey patches around the shoulders are perfectly normal in mature beetroot. Unbroken stems on chard.

STORAGE

Do not wash. Keep in a plastic bag in the refrigerator. Use beet greens and chard within 3 days, roots within 3 weeks. For longer storage, pack roots in peat in a box safe from hard frost but close to 0°C. Their high sugar content is a natural anti-freeze.

MAKING THE MOST OF A SURPLUS

Beetroot keeps well and chard makes good soup. Beetroot is lovely pickled. Do not freeze beetroot or chard.

PINK AND WHITE STRIPED BEETROOT & EGG SALAD

Composed salads are sort of fussy, but if you mix this one up it is ruined.

1 egg per person

1 large or 2 medium striped beetroot
  per person

a few black olives per person

olive oil

fresh dill, finely chopped

- Boil the eggs for about 8 minutes for a slightly moist yolk. Slice them in rounds.
- Slice the beets in thin rounds. Bring enough salted water to cover the beets to the boil, and cook the beetroot until tender, about 7 minutes. Drain, and arrange the beetroot on plates with the eggs and olives, sliced in half or chunks. Sprinkle with olive oil, dill, and salt to taste.

SWISS CHARD & RICE SOUP

*This is my version of an Egyptian soup in Martha Rose Shulman's **Mediterranean Light**. She found the recipe from Claudia Roden's **Book of Middle Eastern Food**.*

SERVES 4

1 onion, peeled and chopped

4 cloves garlic, smashed, peeled, and
  finely chopped

½ tsp cumin seeds

2 tbsp olive oil

500 g Swiss chard, chopped, including
  the stems unless they are very tough

1 x 400-g tin chick peas

100 g rice

1 litre water

300 ml plain yoghurt

juice of ½ lemon

½ tsp salt

- Sauté the onion, 2 cloves of the garlic, and the cumin seeds in the olive oil. When the onion and garlic are soft, add the chard and fry for about 5 minutes.
- Add the chick peas with their juice, the rice, and water. Stir well and simmer until the rice is cooked, about 15 minutes.
- Meanwhile, mix the remaining garlic with the yoghurt and lemon juice.
- Take the soup off the heat and stir in the yoghurt. Season to taste.
- This keeps well for a couple of days in the fridge.

Variations: Spinach, beet greens, or kale would work too. If you use kale, blanch it before you sauté it.

WILD SALMON, COUSCOUS & MARINATED BEETROOTS WITH GREENS

Velvety beet leaves are wonderful with oily salmon. The couscous and fish soak up the pink vinaigrette. It is worth paying more for wild salmon during its brief summer appearance.

SERVES 4

1 bunch beetroot with tops (3–5 beetroots)

1 medium white onion, thinly sliced

2 tbsp best olive oil + a little extra

2 tsp white wine vinegar

1 bay leaf

220 g couscous

2 tbsp fresh chives, chopped

4 wild salmon fillets

- Cut the tops off the beetroot, remove the dead leaves, and trim the roots.
- Slice the beetroot into 1-cm rounds, then slice them into sticks. Chop the greens, including the stem, into pieces about 4–5 cm long. Keep the greens and roots separate.
- Boil enough salted water to cover the beetroot and the greens. Cook the beetroot for 4–6 minutes, until just tender. Add the greens and the onion. Stir, cover and cook for another 5 minutes, until the greens are still bright green but tender. Do not overcook them.
- Drain, reserving a wineglass of the pink stock. Add the olive oil, the white wine vinegar, and salt to taste. Toss, cover, and set aside to marinate for at least 30 minutes or up to 12 hours.
- Bring to the boil 400 ml of salted water with a bay leaf. Add the couscous and stir well. Boil for 1 minute, turn off the heat, and cover. The couscous absorbs water and fluffs up in about 20 minutes. Toss with a teaspoon of olive oil and the chives and check the salt. (This can be made a few hours ahead; you can warm it up with a little water.)
- Brush the salmon with olive oil, then sear it for about 1 minute on both sides, reduce the heat and continue to cook until it is just rose pink in the centre. It keeps cooking on the way to the table.
- Mound couscous, beetroot, and salmon on each plate, pouring the extra beetroot marinade all over. Season to taste.

ROASTED BEETROOT WITH LEMON THYME & GARLIC OIL

1 large or 2 medium beetroot per person

1 tsp lemon thyme per person,
  finely chopped

2 tsp Garlic-in-Oil per person (see p. 219)

- Set the oven to 220°C.
- Slice the beetroot into discs about 1 cm thick, then into chunks or sticks about 1 cm wide.
- Mix together the beetroot, thyme, garlic oil, and salt in a shallow roasting tin. Oil should coat every piece. (This can be done 12 hours ahead, but do not add the salt until just before roasting.)
- Roast for 10 minutes. Then shake pan, reduce the heat to 180°C and roast the beetroot until soft, about 20 minutes. The edges should be brown and slightly shrivelled, but not burnt.

Variations: Try parsnips, swede, or carrots with rosemary or oregano. Onions or leeks cut into chunks are nice. In spring, roast baby beetroot whole with whole garlic cloves. A combination of 1 or 2 vegetables and 1 herb works best.

GOAT'S CHEESE IN RHUBARB CHARD

This makes a wonderful warm starter and takes only minutes to prepare. Save the chard stems for stock.

1 large or 2 small medium rhubarb chard
  leaves per person

2 small rounds 1–cm thick goat's cheese
  per person

olive oil

- Bring to the boil a little salted water. Cook the chard uncovered until it is tender but still bright. It should not be too chewy. Drain.
- Spread the leaves flat, and cut out the white stem and the spine. Place each cheese round on a leaf and season. Wrap the cheese in the leaf, making a snug parcel, and brush the outside with olive oil. If you plan to cook them on a barbecue, spear each parcel with a cocktail stick.
- Grill, bake, or barbecue for 2–5 minutes until the cheese is hot through and slightly creamy, but not dripping. Soft cheese is quicker.

BLUEBERRIES

The perennial blueberry bush is a North American native, but it grows in Britain, too. The smaller wild bilberry, common in Europe, is in the same family. It looks similar, but it is a different species, and it tastes more intense than blueberries.

Blueberries must be very ripe. A good blueberry tastes of more than tangy vitamin C. It is soft and sweet with a strong flavour, much of it in the skin. Compared with home-grown blueberries, imported supermarket berries are often underripe, and too tart even when ripe. That is because the picking machines sweep up half-ripe berries along with ripe ones. The British crop is smaller and usually hand-picked. Blueberries may ripen slightly once picked, but don't bet on it.

The more silver sheen, or bloom, on the berry, the fresher it is and the less it has been handled. An older berry is dark blue, where the bloom has been rubbed off. Size doesn't matter: if the farmer prunes the bushes, the berries are big. If not, they are small. Good-tasting varieties are *Blue Crop* and *Berkeley*.

The blueberry is one of the simplest berries to use. It is sturdy for salads, has no seeds or stems to worry about, and keeps well for several days. This is handy for farmers, too: a ripe blueberry can sit happily on the bush for up to a week, getting sweeter. Unlike raspberries and strawberries, whose flavour deteriorates rapidly, an older blueberry has lost moisture but is still delicious. Blueberries are full of fibre. Similar to cranberries, they can be dried in the oven and used like raisins.

SEASON

Mid-July to August.

WHAT TO LOOK FOR

The 'shoulders' near the stem end should be deep blue, not pink, green, or violet. The tiny petals at the blossom end should be pert, not wilted.
Fresh berries have lots of silvery bloom.

STORAGE

At room temperature for the first day. In the fridge for 3–4 days. Do not wash them until just before you eat.

MAKING THE MOST OF A SURPLUS

Jam, syrup, pie, or summer pudding. Whole blueberries freeze well. Wash and dry them and put them in one layer on a baking sheet. Once frozen, place them in plastic bags. Frozen blueberries work in pancakes and baked goods without defrosting.

BLUEBERRY & ALMOND CRISP

Raspberries and blackberries will also work in this recipe.

SERVES 4–6

500 g blueberries

2 tbsp Vanilla Sugar (see p. 19)

2 tbsp apple or pear juice

¹/₂ tsp cinnamon

a sprinkle of freshly ground nutmeg

1 tbsp cornflour

50 g butter, softened

6 tbsp oats

3 tbsp flour

2 tbsp flaked or crushed almonds

pinch of salt

- Mix the berries with the sugar, juice, spices and cornflour. Leave them to rest for a couple of hours.
- Set the oven to 180ºC. Put the berries in a baking tin. Rub the butter into the dry ingredients. Spread the crumbly topping over the fruit and bake for about 25 minutes, until the berries bubble and the top is crispy.
- Cool slightly to set – when hot, it is too runny – but serve warm.

BLUEBERRY PIE

As American as apple.

SERVES 6–8

700 g blueberries

1 quantity Shortcrust Pastry (makes
   top and bottom crust; see p. 218)

100 g light brown sugar

3 tbsp cornflour

2 tbsp water

¹/₂ tsp cinnamon

vanilla ice cream (optional)

- Set the oven to 180°C.
- Mix the berries with the sugar, cornflour, water, and cinnamon until a glaze forms. Let it stand for 15 minutes.
- Line a 22-cm pie-dish or tin with half of the pastry and fill it with the berries. Lay the pastry lid on top, and pinch it closed between your thumb and forefinger. Make at least 4 crosses in the crust with a knife to let the steam escape when the blueberries collapse.
- Bake the pie for 25 minutes. Move the pie to the other rack in the oven so that it browns evenly and bake for 20 minutes more. Allow it to cool and serve with vanilla ice cream.

LIGHT VANILLA PUDDING
WITH BLUEBERRIES

*Before I lived in England and discovered the decadent native Custard (see p. 218),
we made this light vanilla pudding. It is nice with sugared strawberries, raspberries,
blackberries, and redcurrants. I like it best served cold. In winter, cook frozen berries
with sugar for just 3–4 minutes.*

SERVES 4

300 g blueberries

1 litre milk

5 tbsp cornflour

6 tbsp Vanilla Sugar (see p. 19)

$^1/_2$ tsp salt

2 tsp pure vanilla extract (or 1 tsp
    almond extract)

1–2 knobs butter (optional)

2 tsp sugar for berries, or to taste

- Slice and sugar the berries, then leave them for at least 20 minutes.
- Mix the dry ingredients in a heavy saucepan.
- Add the milk and vanilla, stir well, and then cook gently over a low heat until the mixture is smooth. Then turn up the heat to medium, stirring constantly. Use a slotted spatula: the pudding flows through as you scrape the bottom with the flat edge.
- When it begins to bubble, turn the heat right down and stir for 2 minutes. Remove the pan from the heat and stir in the butter if you want it richer. The pudding is creamy white and pourable. It thickens as it cools. Top with berries.

BAKED BLUEBERRY PUDDING

This is the French **clafoutis***, traditionally made with fresh black cherries. It is easy, light and pretty when the fruit pokes up through the risen batter. The recipe works with any ripe fruit – raspberries, strawberries, blackberries, sliced plums, diced apples or pears. Use the same volume of fruit, about 300 g when diced. For a tart berry, like redcurrants, you may want to add 2 tablespoons sugar. Frozen berries work too – do not defrost them first.*

SERVES 6

4 eggs

6 tbsp sugar

1 tsp vanilla extract

230 g plain flour

generous pinch salt

400 ml milk (use half single cream if
   you prefer it rich)

300 g blueberries, fresh or frozen

icing sugar (optional)

- Set the oven to 200°C.
- Whisk together the eggs, sugar, and vanilla extract until smooth.
- Sift the flour and salt and mix well with the wet ingredients.
- Stir in the milk and whisk well to aerate.
- Butter a baking dish, about 28 x 20 cm.
- Pour in a third of the batter and bake for 3–5 minutes until it is partly set. Otherwise the berries will sink.
- Top with the fruit in one layer, and pour over the remaining batter. Smooth the top and bake for 35 minutes or until set. Dust with the icing sugar and eat immediately, before it settles.

BROCCOLI &
CAULIFLOWER

Broccoli and cauliflower belong to the large *brassica* family whose members – turnips, cabbages, Brussels sprouts, mustards, radishes – have a mustard flavour, from mild to hot. The unpleasant rotten-egg smell is reason enough not to overcook these delicate vegetables, but they also turn mushy and taste bitter.

The moist and temperate British climate is ideal for these cool-weather-loving vegetables, which crop almost all year. Both came from Asia, broccoli (sometimes called calabrese) by way of southern Italy. They are best steamed or stir-fried. For salads or crudités, blanch cauliflower and broccoli very briefly, cool, then dry them. The stems and leaves as well as the florets are edible. Slice the stems and the tender leaves thinly and include them in stir-fries and soups. Mustard seeds are a great addition to *brassica* dishes.

Romanesco Natalino is an Italian broccoli with pale yellow-green pointed buds. *Calabrese* and *De Cicco* produce tender side shoots after the main head is cut. Cauliflower's curving leaves protect it from the sun, blanching it. *Alverda* is green. Purple cauliflower (*Purple Cape*) is milder and turns green when cooked. *Marmalade* stays creamy orange when cooked. *Perfection* and *Idol* are miniature varieties.

In February the first vegetable of the new year appears: purple sprouting broccoli. Very similar to broccoli raab or rapini, it is common in Italy and probably native to the Mediterranean. It is a slender, non-heading broccoli stem with a strong flavour. Every bit is tender and edible – stem, leaf, and buds. The white one, *White Sprouting*, is milder.

The essential rule about the mustard family bears repeating: do not overcook. Depending on the size of the pieces, 2–4 minutes in 1–2 cm boiling salted water, lid off, is plenty.

SEASON

Purple sprouting broccoli: mid-February to mid-April, with late varieties until June. Broccoli: June to frost. Cauliflower: all year.

WHAT TO LOOK FOR

Perky leaves are the best indication of the freshness of the head. In broccoli, a smooth head, not too tight. Each tiny bud should be distinct but closed. When under-mature, the buds are minuscule and the flavour is inferior. When over-mature, the buds start to blossom. Cauliflower should be firm, smooth and heavy for its size.

STORAGE

Cool-weather crops like cool, moist storage, as low as 0°C. In a plastic bag in the fridge, broccoli keeps 2–3 days and cauliflower for up to a week.

MAKING THE MOST OF A SURPLUS

Make soup or purée a large head of broccoli or cauliflower to use it up quickly. You can blanch and freeze florets in bite-sized pieces, but they'll be watery.

PASTA WITH PURPLE SPROUTING BROCCOLI & CHILLIES

Chilli, garlic, and dark greens such as cavolo nero and broccoli are a classic Italian combination.

SERVES 4

6 cloves garlic, smashed, peeled, and finely chopped

2 tbsp olive oil for frying

2 tbsp pine kernels, toasted

600 g purple-sprouting broccoli, washed, trimmed, and cut into bite-sized pieces

500 g short pasta, such as penne

2 tsp dried chilli flakes, or to taste (see p. 153)

2 tbsp best olive oil

- Put the garlic in a bowl with the frying oil.
- In a large dry frying-pan, gently heat the pine kernels, turning frequently, until browned on all sides. Do not let them burn. Set them aside.
- Bring to the boil some salted water in two large saucepans. Blanch the broccoli until barely cooked, not more than 3 minutes. Drain and set it aside.
- Meanwhile, drop the pasta into the other pan. Sauté the garlic and chilli flakes in the pine-kernel pan. The more you heat the chilli in oil, the hotter the dish will become, so if you prefer a milder flavour, add the chilli toward the end of cooking. Put in the broccoli and fry until it is heated through.
- Take the pan off the heat and keep it warm.
- Drain the pasta, reserving a little of the cooking water, then return the pasta to the hot pan. Toss it well with the vegetables and 2 tbsp best olive oil. Season to taste.

Variation: For a side dish, blanch purple-sprouting broccoli in salted water and drain. Sauté a clove of garlic and 2 tablespoons of mustard seeds, then stir in the broccoli and serve.

BROCCOLI WITH
CHICK PEAS & SAGE

This is a favourite ten-minute dinner for one or a side dish for two. It works with asparagus and spinach, too.

1 clove garlic, smashed, peeled, and
  finely chopped

20 sage leaves, stems trimmed

½ tsp chilli pepper flakes

2 tbsp olive oil

1 x 400-g tin chick peas

1 head broccoli, cut into bite-sized pieces

- Gently fry the garlic, sage, and chilli in a tablespoon of the oil until the garlic is soft and the sage is crispy. The longer the chilli is heated in the oil, the hotter the dish will be.
- Meanwhile, drain the chick peas and bring their juice to the boil in a shallow pan. Cook the broccoli until crisp-tender, about 4 minutes.
- With a fork, mash about a third of the chick peas, and add them with the rest to the garlic and sage. Put in the broccoli, any remaining chick-pea juice, and the rest of the olive oil, stir well, and season to taste. For a bigger meal, eat with rice or a pasta that the chick peas can nestle in, like shells.

WARM CAULIFLOWER
WITH MUSTARD VINAIGRETTE

Crunchy mustard seeds go with cauliflower and broccoli – they are all from the same family.

SERVES 2–4

1 medium cauliflower, cut into
  bite-sized pieces

3 tbsp best olive oil

1 tsp white wine vinegar

1 tsp mustard

1–2 tsp honey

1 tsp mustard seeds, yellow or black

- Bring to the boil a large pan of salted water.
- Put the rest of the ingredients, except for the mustard seeds, into a small jar and shake hard.
- Drop the cauliflower into the boiling water and blanch until just tender, 5–7 minutes. Drain and toss with the dressing and the mustard seeds. Season to taste.
- This can be made several hours ahead, but don't add the seeds until just before serving. They get soggy.

BROCCOLI WITH FRESH GARLIC & CANNELLINI BEANS

SERVES 4

1 head fresh or wet garlic, cloves peeled

1 tbsp olive oil

1 tbsp pink peppercorns, crushed between
  your hands

500 g broccoli, trimmed

1 x 400-g tin cannellini beans

1 tbsp best olive oil

- If the garlic cloves are about bean-sized, leave them whole. Halve the big ones.
- Bring some salted water to the boil.
- Meanwhile, heat the olive oil in a frying-pan. Put in the garlic and peppercorns and cook for about 3 minutes, until the oil is flavoured.
- Blanch the broccoli until crisp-tender, about 3 minutes, then drain.
- Add the beans with half of their stock. When the liquid is half gone and the garlic is tender, add the hot broccoli, mix, and remove from heat. Stir in the best olive oil. Season to taste.

CABBAGE, CAVOLO NERO & BRUSSELS SPROUTS

Cabbages, Brussels sprouts, cavolo nero and kale are members of the large *brassica* family, which includes broccoli and mustards. They all contain sulphurous compounds which add little to the flavour, but are responsible for the distinctive odour of overcooked sprouts.

When cut, the *brassicas* also release mild to hot mustard oils. Cabbage and Brussels sprouts aren't the spiciest in the family, so we use pungent relatives like mustard and horseradish to bring out their natural bite. The hot oils in the mustard family are subdued by cooking. That's why raw cabbage makes spicy coleslaw, while steamed cabbage is almost sweet.

Like broccoli and other cool-weather crops, cabbage and Brussels sprouts should be kept cold to inhibit spoilage microbes. Around 0°C is perfect. They need moisture and air, too. Even after harvest, most vegetables are still alive. The cells are still respiring, taking up oxygen and giving out water.

Cabbage is good steamed, braised, baked, stir-fried, shredded, or thrown into soups. Use the darker outer leaves too, which contain more vitamins than the pale heart. *Winnigstadt* is a classic pointy-headed variety. *January King* is green tinged with red. *Ornamental* is spectacular, with pink, green, and white leaves. The red cabbages, like *Red Drumhead*, tend to be denser. Savoy cabbages are crinkly.

At the market you may see Brussels sprouts on their long, thick stalks, because that way they stay fresh longer. Do not do much to sprouts: trim and halve them and then cook in 2–3 cm salted water, uncovered, until tender, about 5 minutes. Then drain and dress them with olive oil and lemon or orange juice while still warm. *Noisette* is a traditional French variety, small, with a nutty flavour.

Cavolo nero, or black cabbage, is Italian. It sends up a spray of long, blue-black crinkly leaves with pale green spines. It has a fine, strong flavour, which stands up well to chillies and garlic. It is delicious steamed, or in *ribollita*, the classic Tuscan soup with bread and cannellini beans. *Tuscan* is a good variety.

Kale is another wonderful dark leafy green for winter. It needs a bit more cooking than cabbage and is delicious in soup. Try the red varieties *Red Russian* and *Redbor*.

SEASON

Cabbage and kale: all year. Brussels sprouts: September to March.
Cavolo nero: August to December.

WHAT TO LOOK FOR

A heavy, tight cabbage with no spots or yellow leaves. Tight sprouts with green leaves, not yellow, on the stalk if possible.

STORAGE

Unwashed, outer leaves on, in a porous bag, as cool as 0°C. The average fridge is 4–7°C. Best eaten within a week. Sprouts on the stalk keep for 2 weeks.

MAKING THE MOST OF A SURPLUS

Cabbage is not worth freezing and tastes terrible tinned, except in sauerkraut. Blanch sprouts in salted water for 1–2 minutes, dry and freeze whole.

MORO'S VILLAGE STEW

*At **Moro**'s restaurant the menu is Spanish with a North African and Islamic gloss. Caraway seeds make this humble stew stand out. The flavour improves if you make it the day before. Kale is a good substitute for cabbage.*

SERVES 4

1 large yellow onion, chopped

2 sticks celery, chopped

2 carrots, peeled and diced small

4 tbsp olive oil

3 large cloves garlic, smashed, peeled, and chopped

2 tsp whole caraway seeds

20 g parsley, trimmed and chopped

1 x 400-g tin whole plum tomatoes, broken up, with juice

³/₄ tsp salt

300 g Savoy or black cabbage, roughly chopped

1 x 400-g tin borlotti or pinto beans with juice

200 g sourdough or other sturdy bread, crust removed

black pepper

best olive oil for drizzling

- In a large saucepan, sauté the onion, celery, and carrots in 2 tablespoons of the oil until the onions are soft and the vegetables begin to turn golden.
- Add the garlic, caraway seeds, and half of the parsley and fry for another 1–2 minutes. Add the tomatoes, their juice, and some salt. Simmer for about 10 minutes.
- Bring to the boil some lightly salted water and blanch the cabbage for 1–2 minutes. Drain, reserving a cup of the cooking water. Add the cabbage and the beans to the pan with the reserved cooking water and the bean juice.
- Cut the bread into large cubes if you are going to serve the stew straightaway.
- Add plenty of black pepper and check the salt.
- When the carrots are tender, stir in the remaining 2 tablespoons of oil and remove the pan from the heat.
- If you make the stew a day ahead, stop now and add the bread when you reheat it.
- Add the bread and a little more water if necessary to reach the right texture. The bread soaks up liquid, but the stew is meant to be thick enough for a spoon to stand up in. Leave it to stand until the bread is soaked through.
- Add the remaining parsley and drizzle with the best olive oil.

COLCANNON WITH BRUSSELS SPROUTS

SERVES 6

1 kg floury potatoes such as *Maris Bard*,
   peeled and quartered
500 g Brussels sprouts, trimmed and
   quartered
5 spring onions, trimmed and chopped
150–200 ml milk (to taste)
1 tbsp butter

- Bring to the boil 2 saucepans of salted water. Put the potatoes into one and cook until tender, about 15 minutes, then mash by hand.
- Drop the sprouts into the other pan and cook until just tender. In the last 20 seconds, add the spring onions. Drain.
- Heat the milk to just short of boiling and add the butter. Mix all the ingredients together, adding the milk bit by bit, depending on how creamy you like it. Check the seasoning and adjust as you are adding the milk.

CAVOLO NERO
WITH CHILLI & GARLIC

SERVES 4

400 g cavolo nero, trimmed and chopped

2 small fresh red chillies, finely sliced

2 tbsp Garlic-in-Oil (see p. 219)

- Steam the cavolo nero in a few centimetres of salted water until just tender, about 2 minutes. Drain.
- In a large pan, sauté the chillies with the Garlic-in-Oil. Add the greens and cook for 1–2 minutes. Season to taste.

BRAISED RED CABBAGE

Another dish that improves with keeping overnight.

SERVES 4–6

1 large head red cabbage, quartered and thinly sliced

2 large crisp eating apples, peeled, cored and thinly sliced

500 ml apple juice

2 tbsp olive oil

50 ml white wine vinegar

2 tbsp honey

1 tsp salt

plenty of pepper

- In a large pan, sauté the cabbage and the apples in the oil over a medium heat until they begin to soften, at least 5 minutes.
- Add the remaining ingredients and simmer until the cabbage is completely soft and the liquid has almost gone, about 20 minutes. Season to taste.

CARROTS

It is worth buying carrots grown without chemicals. To kill carrot fly, some commercial growers use toxic organophosphates, which carrots absorb. That is why the government recommends peeling carrots, especially for children. Peeling removes most post-harvest chemicals – along with fibre and vitamins. Systemic chemicals, which infuse the whole plant, remain. Carrots also absorb the taste of chemicals, so unsprayed carrots may be sweeter. I never peel unsprayed carrots.

Like other cool-weather crops, carrots like the cold. Storage at 0°C is perfect but the fridge will do. Carrots' high sugar and salt content keep them from freezing. Do not keep them near ripening fruit: it makes the carrots bitter and they spoil faster. Like all bright vegetables, they are nutritious, with lots of vitamin C and vitamin A, the precursor to beta-carotene.

Carrots are wonderful raw, especially grated with apples, and are sweet when cooked. Boiling carrots is less satisfactory than roasting: you get more flavour and sweetness by removing water than by adding it.

Baby carrots are lovely because they are new, fresh, and tender, but compared with a mature carrot they have little taste. When carrots get very big, the core is rather woody, but they are still delicious roasted or puréed.

Carrots are grouped by types. Nantes types are the typical, narrow shape. Chautenay types are deeper orange, with broad shoulders. Paris Market types are round, with strong flavour. *Minicor* is a tasty baby carrot. *Touchon Ideal Red* is a 100-year-old French Chautenay type famous for flavour.

The fine-leafed, fragrant carrot family contains 3,000 species and provides a large number of culinary herbs, from dill to coriander to caraway.

SEASON

New carrots in May and June, growing larger through October. Sometimes a second crop of baby carrots in September. Mature carrots from storage through April.

WHAT TO LOOK FOR

Firm, not rubbery, roots, no blemishes. Fresh, green leafy tops. Green 'shoulders' are fine; you can peel that bit.

STORAGE

Brush off the dirt but do not wash. Cut off tops. Store in a porous bag, as cool as 0°C, but the fridge will do. Never store near apples or other ripening fruit. Ethylene released by the fruit makes carrots bitter.

MAKING THE MOST OF A SURPLUS

Even limp carrots are delicious roasted. Frozen slices go soggy, but purée freezes well, and it is useful later for soups and sauces.

BREAST OF CHICKEN WITH SESAME CARROT SALAD

SERVES 4

3–4 large carrots

2 tbsp sesame seeds

2 pieces of ginger, each about 1 cm thick

4 chicken breasts, skinned

3 tbsp rice wine vinegar, or white
  wine vinegar

6 tbsp sesame oil + a little extra

2 sweet juicy eating apples, such as *Gala*
  or *Crowngold*, cored and quartered

1 small red onion, peeled

2 tsp tahini

1 large handful flat parsley

- In a dry frying-pan, toast the sesame seeds, shaking the pan often. Do not let them burn.
- Finely chop one knob of the ginger. Marinate the chicken in 3 tablespoons of the sesame oil, 2 tablespoons of the rice wine vinegar and the ginger.
- Grate carrots, saving any juice.
- Cut the apples and the onion in large chunks and process until they are in pea-sized pieces. Separately, process parsley, onion, and ginger until fine.
- Put the carrot juice, the remaining sesame oil, 1 tablespoon of the rice wine vinegar, and the tahini in a jar. Shake well. Toss the salad ingredients in the dressing. Add salt and pepper to taste.
- Heat a little sesame oil in a pan and sear the chicken on both sides. Reduce the heat until it is cooked through.
- Put some salad on each plate and top it with a chicken breast. Sprinkle over some of the sesame seeds and a little more sesame oil.

Variation: Use salmon instead of chicken. The restaurant method for cooking fish fillets is easy: butter or oil a hot frying-pan, sear each side for 2 minutes, then put the frying-pan in a hot oven for 3 minutes. It should be crispy on the outside and just pink in the middle.

WINTER SALAD

SERVES 2–4

3 large carrots, grated

2 medium sweet apples, grated

1–2 small red radishes

2 tbsp apple juice

1 clove garlic, smashed, peeled, and
  finely chopped

2 tbsp best olive oil

salt and pepper

- Mix everything together thoroughly, then season generously. Leave the salad to stand for 30 minutes to allow the flavours to meld.

CARROT & GARLIC TAPAS

We ate plates of this in Seville. They sit on the bar in large bowls, swimming in the dressing, which is almost a marinade. When the carrots are gone, use up the leftover dressing on salad.

SERVES 4–6

6 tbsp olive oil

4 tbsp sherry vinegar

800 g carrots, sliced

2 large cloves garlic, smashed, peeled, and finely chopped (or more to taste)

- Mix together the oil, vinegar, and garlic, and leave it to stand: the longer it rests, the more garlicky the carrots.
- Boil the carrots in salted water until just tender, about 5 minutes. Drain.
- Coat the warm carrots completely in the vinaigrette. Check the seasoning and leave for at least 1 hour, preferably overnight. Remove the carrots from the dressing with a slotted spoon so that they are not too oily. Eat at room temperature on small plates with cocktail sticks or as a salad.

ROASTED CARROTS WITH GARLIC & THYME

Carrots are also delicious with sage and rosemary (chop them very finely). Or try whole garlic cloves, peeled and cut in half if very large.

SERVES 2–4

500–600 g carrots

2 tbsp fresh thyme, finely chopped

2 tbsp olive oil

2 large cloves garlic, smashed, peeled, and finely chopped

- Set the oven to 200°C. For an alternative to round slices, hold the carrot at the fat end, cut off a diagonal slice, spin carrot a quarter turn, and cut another slice. Continue as if sharpening a pencil. It is essential that the pieces are of equal thickness.
- Cover the thyme and garlic with oil for 30 minutes if you have time. Mix well with the carrots, salt and roast for 10 minutes, or until the edges begin to brown. Shake the pan if they are sticking and turn down the heat to 180°C and roast for another 15–20 minutes, until the carrots are soft.

GINGER CARROT CAKE

The more mature the carrots, the stronger the flavour. This is not too sweet and makes a good breakfast.

SERVES 6–8

450 g carrots, sliced

2 x 2 cm piece of ginger, finely chopped

250 g flour

2 tsp baking powder

1 tsp salt

1 tsp allspice

1 tsp cinnamon

3 large eggs, separated

150 ml honey

75 ml vegetable or light olive oil

1 tsp vanilla extract

- Boil the carrots with half the ginger. When they are soft, purée with a spoonful of cooking water until smooth. You should have about 400 ml of purée.
- Set oven to 200°C and oil a tin (about 20 cm in diameter and 5 cm deep).
- Thoroughly mix the dry ingredients in a large bowl.
- In another bowl, whisk the carrot purée, remaining ginger, 2 egg yolks, honey, oil, and vanilla.
- Beat all the egg whites until stiff.
- Combine the carrot mixture with the dry ingredients quickly but thoroughly.
- Fold in the egg whites, pour in the tin, and bake at 200 °C for 15 minutes. Reduce heat to 180°C and bake for about 40 more minutes – until a knife comes out clean. Remove cake from the tin and cool on a rack. Dust with icing sugar.

Tip: To get every drop of honey, measure the oil first, coating the inside of the measuring cup. Then use the cup for the honey; it will slide out easily.

CELERY &
CELERIAC

Celery provides crucial flavour in stocks and soups, but it is also delicious as the primary ingredient, especially when braised. Farmers' market celery is strongly flavoured; supermarket celery is milder because it is usually stripped of its dark green outer stems and leaves. The white and yellow inner sticks – the heart – are milder and more tender. If the larger sticks are fibrous, pull off the strings.

Celery comes in green, red, and self-blanching or white varieties. For the paler milder one, farmers often blanch green celery, depriving it of light by heaping soil high around it. *Golden Self Blanching* is creamy white and mild without being covered. *Giant Red* has dark red stalks which go pink when blanched, and an excellent flavour. Like parsnips and other cold-weather crops, some celeries taste better after a frost.

Celeriac, or celery root, is a gnarled, tufted white root with leaves looking a bit like flat parsley. It has the strong taste of ribbed celery, but it is a different plant. Both were cultivated from wild celery in the sixteenth century. It needs thorough scrubbing and peeling; grit gets into all the crevices. Celeriac discolours quickly: to stop it turning brown, drop it in water with some lemon juice as you prepare it.

Celeriac is delicious raw in salads. It is nicer still if blanched briefly first. After grating, drop it into boiling water with some lemon juice, drain, then plunge into cold water, and dry it before dressing it. It is also good in purées and soups and suits potatoes and cream. *Celeri Rémoulade* is the classic dish: julienne or grate the celeriac and dress it with Mayonnaise (see p. 218), mustard, and finely chopped parsley. A hard-boiled egg and tarragon vinegar are nice accents. *Mars* is a good variety.

SEASON

Celery: July to December, or until frost.
Celeriac: from early September, from storage until February.

WHAT TO LOOK FOR

Fresh, green leaves on celery and shiny ribs. Celeriac should be smallish, heavy, with no soft spots.

STORAGE

Unwashed, in a porous bag at about 0°C or in the fridge.
Celery and celeriac keep about two weeks.

MAKING THE MOST OF A SURPLUS

Celery doesn't freeze well, but Celery Soup does (see p. 79).
Celeriac: peel, dice, blanch for 3–4 minutes, and freeze.

CELERIAC RISOTTO

A delicious autumn and winter dish. Eat it with Roasted Onion Squash with Sage (see p. 170). Celeriac is strong. If you love the taste, as I do, use 300 g. If you prefer small doses, use 100 g.

SERVES 4–8

100–300 g celeriac (to taste), peeled, and finely chopped

3 large cloves garlic, smashed, peeled, and finely chopped

1/2 yellow onion, finely chopped

3 tbsp olive oil + a little extra (optional)

400 g Arborio or other short-grained rice

1.5 litres chicken or vegetable stock

2 glasses white wine

1 tsp salt

4–5 tbsp freshly grated cheese, such as Pecorino or Parmesan

2 tbsp chives, finely chopped

• In a large, heavy-bottomed pan, sauté the vegetables in olive oil until they are soft and translucent, 5–7 minutes.

• Bring the stock to the boil and keep it hot.

• Add the rice to the vegetable pan and stir well to coat it in oil. Add half of the wine, turn up the heat, stir until it is absorbed, then pour in the rest. Add the salt.

• Reduce the heat and add the stock in small amounts as it is absorbed, constantly scraping the bottom, about 20 minutes. When the rice is tender but not mushy and the sauce is creamy, stir in the cheese. Season to taste and top with chives.

Proper risotto is *al dente*, but I like it softer than that. Most recipes call for 400 g rice to 1 litre of stock. I use the full 1.5 litres; you may not. Taste it, or cut a grain open. The outside should be creamy and there should be barely a kernel of white in the centre. Risotto stiffens and dries a bit between pan and table, so don't worry if it is a bit wet when the rice is done. Hot plates help.

BRAISED CELERY WITH SAGE

A winter dish: sage grows all year, and celery is one of the few green vegetables at Christmas. Thyme and oregano, or a mix of both, would work too.

SERVES 4

1 onion, peeled and chopped

1 large leek, trimmed, washed, and sliced
   in narrow rounds

3 tbsp olive oil

2 cloves garlic, smashed, peeled, and
   finely chopped

2 tsp fresh sage, or 1 tsp dried

2 bay leaves

1 large head of celery, trimmed, and cut
   into 4-cm pieces

generous glass white wine

300–400 ml vegetable or chicken stock

- Sweat the onion and the leek in the oil until they are translucent. Add the garlic and herbs and sauté gently.
- Put in the celery, stir to coat, turn up the heat and add the wine. When it steams off, add the stock, cover, and reduce the heat. Cook until the celery is tender and stock is almost absorbed, about 25 minutes. Each serving needs a bit of stock. Check salt, remembering that both celery and stock are salty.

CELERY SOUP

SERVES 4

1 litre vegetable or chicken stock

2 tbsp flour

2 medium yellow onions, chopped

2 tbsp olive oil

2 bunches celery, about 800 g trimmed

3 large cloves garlic, smashed, peeled,
   and chopped

500 g potatoes, peeled and chopped

scant ¼ tsp ground celery seed

1 tsp mustard (optional)

- Bring the stock to the boil. In a small saucepan, make a smooth paste with about 150 ml hot stock and the flour.
- Sauté the onions in the oil in a large pot. Add the celery and the garlic and continue to sauté until they soften, about 5 minutes. Add the flour paste, potatoes, hot stock, celery seed, and mustard.
- Simmer until the celery and potatoes are completely soft, about 25 minutes.
- Purée the mixture and dilute it with water to make 4 generous bowls of light green soup – otherwise it will be too thick and strong. Check the seasoning, remembering that both the stock and the celery are salty. This soup freezes well.

COURGETTES & SUMMER SQUASH

Courgettes and summer squashes are actually fruits, not vegetables. We eat them immature, before the seeds are capable of reproducing. At this point, the vegetables are large enough to have flavour, but the seeds and rind are still tender. A marrow is allowed to reach a more mature stage, with big seeds and a tough skin. A winter squash reaches full ripeness; the rind is hard for long keeping, and the seeds are viable. All three – marrow, summer and winter squashes – are in the *cucurbit* family. As with beans, we pick its members at different stages.

Do not make a fetish of baby squashes. They are tender but have little flavour. Perfect summer squash is not merely a question of size but of maturity. As with so many vegetables, the key to perfection lies not in our hands but in the farmer's. Squash consists mostly of water, loves hot weather, and grows fast, so the farmer picks every day. Careful picking catches squash at exactly the right moment. A day late, and it is over-mature. Conditions matter: a larger courgette that grew quickly, unchecked by drought or cold, is as tender as a tiny one – or more so, if the little one grew slowly with too little rain.

If not size, then what clues can the customer follow? Perfect summer squashes are shiny and sticky, with tender skin. Picked recently and carefully handled, they still have small hairs. Courgettes are bright, not dull green, and summer squash is pale, not dark yellow, with no warts.

Courgettes come in green, golden (*Gold Rush, Taxi*) and pale green, almost white. For best flavour, try *Clarion*, pale green and slightly bulbous at one end, the Lebanese *Opal*, the ridged *Romanesco*, or the round *Tondo Chiaro de Nizza*. Yellow summer squash is shorter, drumstick-shaped and milder. There is also yellow crookneck, with a narrow, swan-like neck. The adorable patty-pan (sometimes called cymling) is a scalloped disc. Golden or pale green, it should also be picked when pale, shiny, and sticky, not dull.

SEASON

June to early October.

WHAT TO LOOK FOR

Shiny, bright green and yellow skin, not dull or dark. No scratches means they've been handled carefully. No warts. The cut stem of very recently picked squash oozes a pale sticky goo.

STORAGE

These hot-weather crops like to be kept at about 10°C, a bit warmer than the average fridge. The refrigerator will not harm them, but neither will a shady, cool spot in the larder or kitchen. Keep dry, and use in 3–4 days.

MAKING THE MOST OF A SURPLUS

Steam, then purée, and stir into milk or stock for soup. Summer squashes do not freeze well.

YELLOW SQUASH WITH
CHICK PEAS & ANCHOVIES

*The anchovy oil makes this warm salad salty, so bear this in mind when seasoning it.
It is delicious served over pasta. If you find the anchovy oil too strong, use olive oil
instead. Try the recipe with yellow courgettes instead of the squash.*

SERVES 2

2 yellow summer squash, chopped
   with diagonal rotation method (see below)
1 chilli pepper, finely chopped, no seeds
1 x 50-g tin anchovies in oil, rinsed and
   drained, oil reserved
200 g chick peas, drained (half 400-g tin)
best olive oil
good Parmesan for grating

- Blanch the squash in salted water for 2 minutes, then drain.
- Sauté the chilli in the anchovy oil. Add the squash and chick peas and stir quickly to
  heat through.
- Top with olive oil to taste and grated cheese. Serve warm.

To cut cylindrical courgettes and summer squash in different shapes: slice the ends off the courgette.
Cut a corner off one end. Give the courgette a quarter turn and cut off another corner. Keep rotating
and chopping as if you were sharpening a pencil to a point. Makes a nice chunky diagonal shape.

PASTA PRIMAVERA

SERVES 4

500 g runner beans, strings removed,
   cut into thirds
600 g yellow, green and white courgettes
   or summer squash (about 4), chopped
   with diagonal rotation method
   (see opposite)
1 small fresh chilli pepper, finely chopped
2 tbsp Garlic-in-Oil (see p. 219)
400 g short pasta
good cheese for grating
1 large handful lime or Genovese basil,
   leaves only, chopped
olive oil (optional)

- Blanch the vegetables in boiling salted water, about 2 minutes. Drain, keeping the water for the pasta, and set aside.
- Sauté chilli with the Garlic-in-Oil and remove it from the heat.
- Bring to the boil a large pan of salted water and cook the pasta.
- At the last minute, add the vegetables to the chillies and sauté briefly until warm through. Stir into the pasta, with the cheese and the basil, and perhaps a little olive oil to make it slippery. Season to taste.

LAYERED COURGETTE & AUBERGINE TART

Buy vegetables of equal diameter.

SERVES 4–6

1 sheet frozen puff pastry, 200 g, defrosted

500 g courgettes

400 g small aubergines, preferably the
   narrow Japanese kind

300 g small tomatoes, sliced

3 tbsp olive oil

2 tbsp pine kernels

about 15 basil leaves, shredded

1 tbsp best olive oil

- Roll out the pastry to about 20 cm x 40 cm. Lay the pastry flat on a baking sheet with no sides. Turn up the edges less than half a centimetre, then make tiny cuts all the way round perpendicular to the edge with a knife. This makes a nice puffy edge.
- Set the oven to 180°C. Slice the courgettes and aubergines into rounds of equal thickness. Toss or brush them with the olive oil in a baking dish. Do not let the aubergines soak up all the oil. Salt and then bake until they are almost soft, about 20 minutes. Shake the pan once or twice to prevent sticking.
- Layer the vegetables and the tomatoes in close rows running lengthways down the pastry. Leave a border 1½ cm wide of uncovered pastry; this is where it puffs. Each slice should overlap the next by no more than half. In each row, alternate 2 vegetables. The layer must be thin, or the pastry will be soggy.
- Bake at 200°C for 30 minutes, until the vegetables are roasted and the pastry is puffed and golden.
- Toast the pine kernels in a dry frying-pan until golden. Top the tart with the basil and the pine kernels and drizzle the best olive oil on top. Eat warm or cold.

CUCUMBERS

Cucumbers consist mostly of water, but they shouldn't be tasteless. Supermarket cucumbers are often grown under glass with only water and liquid feed for nourishment, but vegetables should get their flavour from soil minerals, and probably also from the slight stress of rain, wind, and direct sun – all things hothouse plants do not get. Even if cucumbers are grown outdoors, the variety must be a tasty one. Over-irrigating and over-fertilising are shortcuts to higher yields, but produce watery fruit.

A perfect cucumber has thin skin, firm, crisp flesh, tender seeds, and a distinct flavour, almost of melon. If you do not know the taste of cucumber, try salad burnett, an herb with a pronounced cucumber flavour.

There are smooth, glasshouse cucumbers and outdoor, or ridged types. The best-tasting cucumber – a small, Middle Eastern variety called *Beit Alpha* – is grown both ways. Tender, with a thin skin and small seed cavity, it is best at about 15 cm long. The small green and white striped ones, sometimes called gherkins, are bred for pickling but delicious in salads. *National Gherkin* and *Fanfare* are excellent. Long, slim, ribbed Asian varieties, so-called Burpless, and bitter-free types also have great flavour.

As with their fellow *cucurbits*, the summer squashes, maturity is not merely a question of size. Shape is more critical for cucumbers. When viewed from the end, a perfectly picked cucumber is slightly triangular. A bulbous cucumber was picked too late. It will have thick skin, tough seeds, and bland flesh.

There is no need to peel cucumbers. Their light taste goes with spices, sour ingredients like yoghurt, and sweet flavours – they are lovely with a honey vinaigrette. In green salads, I think cucumbers are overrated, but in chopped salads, gazpacho, and salsas they are wonderful.

SEASON

Under glass: as early as May; June to September. Gherkins: July.

WHAT TO LOOK FOR

Shape is slightly triangular when viewed from the end, not bulging. Spines indicate recent picking and careful handling. Firm, not rubbery.

STORAGE

Like their hot-weather-loving relative the courgette, cucumbers like to be at about 10°C, a bit warmer than the average fridge. The refrigerator will not harm them, but neither will a shady, cool spot in the kitchen or larder. Keep them dry. Use in 3–4 days.

MAKING THE MOST OF A SURPLUS

More cucumber salad, or cold cucumber soup (purée it with yoghurt and mint). Pickles, if you are ambitious.

MY GRANDMOTHER'S CUCUMBER SALAD

When cucumbers come in at the farm, we eat this five times a week. Later we add tomatoes, then red peppers. Cut the cucumbers paper-thin. Make plenty of dressing: it is almost a marinade, and the salad will be better if allowed to stand an hour before eating. You can play with the sweet-sour balance to discover what's best for you.

SERVES 4

500 g gherkins, sliced very thin
  (or cucumbers)
500 g tomatoes, sliced in chunks
1 large onion, sliced very thin

For the dressing
3 tbsp best olive oil
2 tbsp + 1 tsp cider vinegar
2 tbsp + 1 tsp honey

- Put the dressing ingredients in a jar and shake well. Mix all ingredients and leave to stand for at least 30 minutes. Add salt and plenty of black pepper to taste.
- Salt and honey draw out the vegetable juices, so serve the salad in bowls at room temperature, dipping bread into the dressing.

Variation: Add 1 red bell pepper, finely sliced, or skip the tomatoes and add 3 tablespoons of fresh dill, finely chopped, instead.

CUCUMBER MINT DIP

Like raita, this goes with lentils and rice. It is also good for dipping toasted pitta bread, or for dressing a potato or egg salad. Eat it with poached fish or chicken or with baked aubergine. If you have no mint, use chives, spring onions, or green chillies.

SERVES 4

1 clove garlic, smashed and peeled
1 shallot, peeled
1 tbsp olive oil
1/2 tsp ground cayenne (or to taste)

large handful fresh mint
250 ml Greek yoghurt
300 g cucumbers, in large chunks

- In the food-processor, blend the garlic, shallot, oil, cayenne, mint, and 2 tablespoons of the yoghurt until almost smooth.
- Add the cucumbers and the rest of the yoghurt and continue to process until mostly smooth, with bits of cucumber still detectable. Season to taste.

SEARED SALMON
WITH CUCUMBER DRESSING

SERVES 2

2 fillets salmon

2 tbsp dill, finely chopped

1 medium cucumber, diced small

½ clove garlic, smashed, peeled, and
  finely chopped

2 tbsp yoghurt

1 tbsp best olive oil + a little extra
  for the fish

rock salt

- Mix cucumber and dill with the garlic, yoghurt, oil, salt and pepper.
- The chef's way to pan-roast fish is foolproof. Set the oven to 200°C. Brush each fillet with a little oil. Heat a film of oil in an ovenproof frying-pan. Sear both sides of the salmon quickly over a high heat, then reduce the heat and cook for 1 minute. Put it in the oven for 3–5 minutes to finish. The centre should just be rosy.
- Top with the cucumber salsa and sprinkle salt on top. The salt should be crunchy and distinct.

CURRANTS & GOOSEBERRIES

Britain is berry country, and currants and gooseberries – the ribes, hence Ribena – are especially well suited to its climate. The easy-going blackcurrant, a northern European native, even tolerates partial shade. For the grower, red-, white- and pinkcurrants are similar, while the blackcurrant needs quite different treatment. For the cook, there are slight differences. All currants are delicious in jam and summer pudding, but red-, white- and pinkcurrants are smaller and more delicate. Redcurrants are strong-tasting and tart, while whitecurrants have a delicate flavour. Red-, pink-, and whitecurrants are lovely in salads or even on their own, but the blackcurrant is almost always cooked. The blackcurrant is a bigger, sturdier berry with a strong taste, almost of cinnamon.

Currants are relatively delicate. At market, red- and whitecurrants should still be clustered on the strig – the little stalk. They should be kept perfectly dry and must be as ripe as possible.

Gram for gram, the blackcurrant has almost eight times as much vitamin C as an orange. Red- and pinkcurrants and gooseberries have some vitamin C, whitecurrants none. *Jonkhar van Tets* (red), *Ben Connan* (black), and *Blanka* (white) have excellent flavour. *Pink Champagne* is a lovely translucent rose.

In *Soft Fruit Growing*, Raymond Bush laments the gooseberry's decline. 'Exotic and out-of-season fruits have reduced the ripe and succulent gooseberry to the position of a nonentity in the greengrocer's window.' (*Soft Fruit Growing for the Amateur*, Penguin.) Bush was writing in 1944. In fact, the privations of war caused a small renaissance in home gooseberry growing.

Gooseberries come green, white, almost black, yellow, and deep pink. *Rokula* (red), *Leveller* (yellow), and *Invicta* (green) are known for flavour and sweetness. Gooseberries have lots of vitamin A. When ripe, they are nice in fruit salads in small quantities. Cooked, they have a slightly smoky taste and make delicious pie, or a classic sauce for oily fish such as mackerel. To make the sauce, boil gooseberries until they split and soften, run them through a sieve, and add sugar, lemon juice, and butter.

SEASON

Currants: June to August. Gooseberries: June and July.

WHAT TO LOOK FOR

Shiny, firm berries, the redder or blacker the better. Ripe white ones are slightly creamy. Lift up a cluster to see how ripe they are. Careless pickers may include half-ripes.

STORAGE

Leave currants on the stalk. Spread blackcurrants and gooseberries in one or two layers on kitchen paper and refrigerate. Use within 2–3 days.

MAKING THE MOST OF A SURPLUS

Black or Whitecurrant Jelly (p. 93), Summer Pudding (p. 92), or Sorbet (p. 94). These berries freeze well, either whole (wash and stem, freeze in one layer on

SUMMER PUDDING

Individual Summer Puddings are pretty and do not collapse. Use a tulip-shaped glass with a rounded bottom that holds about 300 ml. If you use a single, large bowl, line it with clingfilm, leaving plenty hanging over the edge, before lining it with bread. The pudding will pop out intact. The secret to purple-drenched bread: dip it in the syrup before lining the glasses or bowls.

Currants are the classic Summer Pudding berry, but do not use more than one third blackcurrants. Their flavour is too strong.

SERVES 8

1.5 kg mixed berries (strawberries, red- and blackcurrants, blueberries, raspberries, blackberries)
1 vanilla pod
150–175 g sugar (depending on taste and tartness of berries)

250 ml water
1 large day-old white loaf, or 2 medium (the more bread, the easier to fit the pieces for lining)
whipped cream to serve

- The day before eating, pick over and trim the berries. Set aside about a quarter of them. You will add half of these to the cooked berries and keep a few to garnish.
- Split the vanilla pod and scrape its seeds into a saucepan. Add the pod, the main quantity of berries, two-thirds of the sugar, and the water.
- Mix and heat gently until the berries collapse, 5–10 minutes. Add the remaining sugar to taste. Cool and strain.
- Line a bowl with clingfilm. Remove the crusts from the bread. Make a round slice for the bottom (or tiny round slices for the glasses). Cut to fit to line the container, leaving no gaps.
- Dunk the bread slices in the syrup until they are purple on all sides, then line the bowl (or glasses) leaving no gaps.
- Mix all but 100 ml of the remaining syrup, cooked berries, and fresh berries. Remove the vanilla pod. Fill the bowl (or glasses) with fresh berries, packing it well. Top with bread slices. The bread can be higher than the rim of the bowl, but must fit snugly.
- Wrap the overhanging clingfilm cross the top of the bowl, cover with a baking tin and weight it with tins. (Place glasses close together on a tray, cover with clingfilm and top with a tin to weight it.) Chill overnight.
- Remove the clingfilm, invert the pudding(s) on the serving dish(es), and gently ease out.
- Garnish with the reserved fresh berries, any leftover syrup, and whipped cream.

BLACK OR WHITECURRANT JELLY

An Eliza Acton recipe from 1845, slightly more wobbly than commercial jelly. Jam is cloudy, but jelly should be clear.

MAKES about 1.5 kg

900 kg white- or blackcurrants

1 kg sugar

- Wash and pick over the berries. The odd stem is fine. Mix them with the sugar and heat gently. When it bubbles, simmer for exactly 8 minutes – use a timer. Add a little water only if necessary.
- Line a colander with muslin and set it over a large bowl. Pour in the berries and let them drain overnight. Do not squeeze the cloth: this makes the jelly cloudy.
- Put the syrup into clean jars.

GOOSEBERRY PIE

To me, gooseberries taste slightly smoky. If you have a sweet tooth, use 300 g sugar.

SERVES 6–8

700 g gooseberries

1 quantity Shortcrust Pastry recipe, which
    makes top and bottom crusts (see p. 218)

250 g sugar

3 tbsp cornflour

2 tbsp water

- Set the oven at 180°C. Mix the gooseberries with the sugar, cornflour and water until a glaze forms, then let it stand for 15 minutes.
- Line the tin with pastry then pour in the gooseberries. Lay the pastry lid over the gooseberries, pinching the edges between thumb and forefinger to close. Make at least 4 crosses in the crust to let the steam escape.
- Bake for 45 minutes at 180°C. After 20 minutes, put the pie on the other shelf in the oven, so that it browns evenly.

GOOSEBERRY APPLE SORBET

Because this does not contain alcohol, which makes sorbet slushy, the texture is much smoother when it is frozen in an ice-cream maker.

SERVES 4

700 g gooseberries, stems and brown
  flower-caps removed
500 ml apple juice
125–150 ml sugar

- Bring all the ingredients to the boil, reduce the heat, and cook until the gooseberries are soft, about 20 minutes.
- Let it cool then purée until it is completely smooth. Strain out the tiny seeds if you like. Chill then freeze in an ice-cream maker. (Or see Blackcurrant Granita opposite, for freezing by hand.)
- If you are not eating it now, put it into the freezer. Allow it to soften in the fridge for 20–30 minutes before eating. Serve with sliced strawberries.

BLACKCURRANT GRANITA

Granita is like sorbet, but with a coarser texture. The wine prevents it from freezing fully, so the more you use, the slushier and more alcoholic it will be.

SERVES 8–10

1 kg blackcurrants	125–150 ml fruity red wine
200 g sugar	a sprinkle of cinnamon

- Wash and pick over the blackcurrants and remove the stems. Put them into a saucepan with the sugar and simmer until the berries are well cooked, at least 20 minutes. Add a little water only if necessary.
- For a smoother texture, strain the berries and use only the syrup. Otherwise, purée the stewed berries with the cinnamon and the wine until they are very smooth. Chill and freeze in an ice-cream maker, or use the following method:
- Spread in a wide, shallow baking tin and freeze. Stir every hour with a whisk to stop ice crystals forming – the more you stir the better. Eat when the consistency is right.
- If you are not eating the granita the day you made it, remove from the freezer and put in the fridge for 20–30 minutes to soften before serving.

FENNEL

Aniseed-flavoured fennel used to be found mostly in good Italian delis and the supermarket, but now the heavy white bulb is often grown locally. It is one of the easiest vegetables: it slices beautifully into crescent shapes. It is lovely sautéed, baked, braised, or steamed, and delicious sliced thinly in salads or dipped in hummus or Broad Bean Paste (see p. 42). It goes with light flavours, like peas, as well as stronger ones, like Butternut Squash Purée (see p. 170). It adds great flavour to stock, especially fish. Like the onion, it turns sweet when cooked. Fennel suits potatoes, pasta, and white fish like sea bass.

Florentine fennel is the plant that forms a white bulb above ground. The centre is more tender than the outside. With more mature bulbs, you may need to discard the outer layers. Cut off the top stalks, then cut the bulb in half, lay it flat, and slice it, popping the round core from the inner pieces. Add the stalks, core, and tough outer layers, which are full of flavour, to stocks or soups, or stuff them into the cavity of roasted fish or chicken.

Common or green fennel is the herb, and comes with leaves only. It is sometimes bronze-coloured. The bulb should come with green ferny leaves, too, which you can use as the herb. They are lovely cooked with the fennel, or added to soups, salads, and purées (Pea & Fennel Purée, p. 144). Chopped, they dry beautifully on a saucer, and take on a new flavour. Fennel is a good substitute for dill, nice on potatoes and cucumbers. Pernod is a natural match.

SEASON

Baby fennel from June. Main crop, July to September.

WHAT TO LOOK FOR

Fresh, green, ferny leaves, tight head, and crisp stalks. No brown spots on the white ribs. Heavy for its size. Very small ones are more tender.

STORAGE

Do not wash or remove tops. Keep dry in a porous bag in the fridge for 4–5 days. Use leaves quickly, or chop and dry them. If the bulb goes a bit brown, the inside is usually still fine.

MAKING THE MOST OF A SURPLUS

Doesn't freeze well. Boil it, then purée and add to potato or other creamy soups.

WARM TUNA SALAD IN BALSAMIC VINEGAR MARINADE

The larger amounts make a more substantial meal.

1/2–1 tuna fillet per person

2 cloves garlic, smashed, peeled and
   chopped

1/2–1 large fennel bulb per person,
   finely chopped, leaves reserved

1 tbsp olive oil

For the marinade
(enough for 1–2 tuna fillets)

100 ml balsamic vinegar

2 tbsp rice wine vinegar

1 tbsp olive oil

For the dressing
(enough for 2 servings)

2 tsp balsamic vinegar

2 tbsp olive oil

- Put the marinade ingredients into a bowl and stir thoroughly. Add salt and pepper.
- Rinse the tuna, dry it, then marinate it with the garlic for at least 2 hours. Turn half-way through. The longer it marinates, the less cooking time required. The acidic vinegar 'cooks' the fish.
- Mix the dressing and season it.
- Sauté the fennel in the olive oil until soft, but do not let it brown. Keep it warm.
- Remove the garlic bits from the tuna and sear the fish briefly on both sides – leave it as rare in the middle as you like it. Slice it into long thin strips, against the grain – pink ribbons with white edges. Pile the warm fennel on the plate, add the tuna strips, and drizzle over the dressing. Do not toss. Sprinkle over the finely chopped fennel leaves. Eat warm.

CRAB SALAD WITH FENNEL LEAVES

Another dish that improves with keeping overnight.

SERVES 2

½ small fennel bulb with leaves

1 large dressed crab

2 tbsp best olive oil

a squeeze of lemon juice

- Slice the fennel very, very thinly. Otherwise it will be too chunky for the crab. Finely chop the leaves.
- Mix everything together and check the seasoning.

BAKED FENNEL & POTATOES

SERVES 6

1 kg fennel, thinly sliced

4 large cloves garlic, peeled and sliced
  in long slivers

3 tbsp olive oil

1 kg potatoes, thinly sliced

- Set the oven to 180°C. Sauté the fennel and garlic in the olive oil until mostly soft, 10–12 minutes. Add the potatoes, stir well, and fry for a few minutes. Season with salt and pepper.
- Lay the vegetables in a baking dish, one or two layers deep. Bake until soft, about 30 minutes.

SEA BASS BAKED IN
FENNEL & PERNOD

The Duke of Cambridge *in Islington was London's first all-organic gastro pub. The menu is seasonal and unpretentious. Farmers at the Islington market around the corner supply the kitchen. (See also Mushroom Stew with Crostini, p. 128.)*

SERVES 4

2–3 small or 1 large fennel bulb per person,
  with leaves, thinly sliced
2 tbsp butter or olive oil per person
  (or more to taste)
200 ml Pernod per person
1–2 tbsp cream per person (optional)
1 whole sea bass per person, head
  removed, if you prefer, and cleaned

- Sauté the fennel in the oil or butter. Slowly add the Pernod, sprinkle in some salt, and cover. Reduce the heat and simmer until the fennel is soft. For a richer sauce, add a spoonful of cream per serving.
- Set the oven to 200°C. Rinse the fish and season it lightly inside and out.
- Spread a large piece of greaseproof paper for each fish on a baking sheet. Spread a layer of fennel on the paper, then the fish. Fill the fish with fennel, and lay more fennel on top. Spoon over any stock, gather up the paper and staple it closed, making it as airtight as possible.
- Bake for about 15 minutes. Take it to the table sealed.

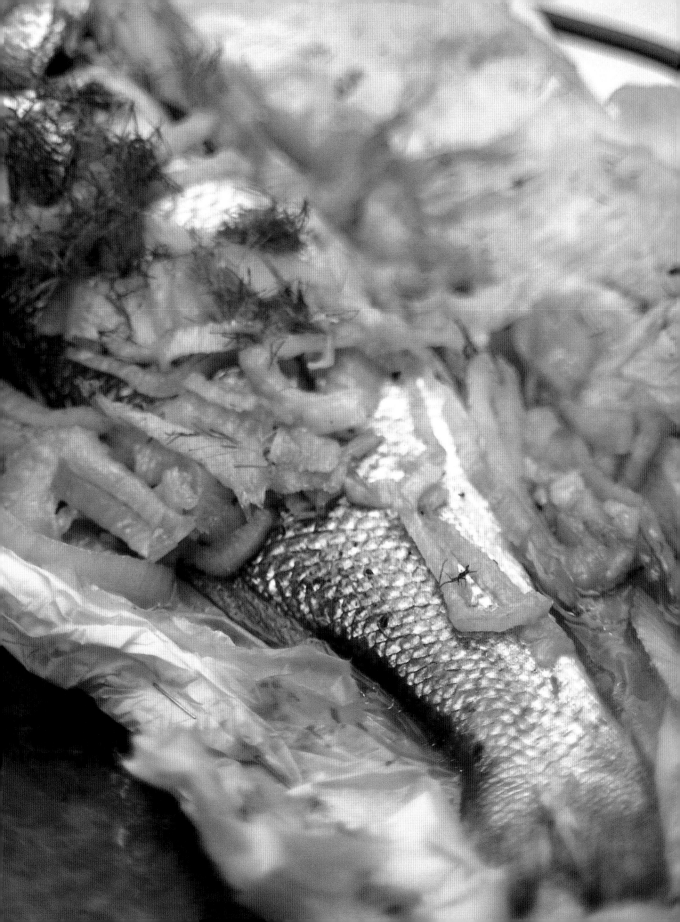

GARLIC & ONIONS

Garlic comes in two types, stiff-necked and soft-necked. Soft-necked varieties are more common commercially: they are easier to grow, yield more, and store well. Garlic gourmands prefer stiff-necked varieties, which have more distinctive flavours and cloves of equal size.

Printanor is a basic soft-necked garlic bred for Britain's climate. Elephant or Spanish garlic is technically a kind of leek, large and mild. It is easy to modify garlic's heat. Garlic's volatile oils are activated by breaking the tissue and muted by exposure to air. The mildest option is roasting whole cloves. Next is peeling and slicing, followed by chopping in large pieces, then in tiny ones. For the most pungency, smash an unpeeled clove against a cutting board with a blunt object. Remove the peel, then pound it with rock salt with a mortar and pestle. Garlic is a powerful antibiotic and reduces blood pressure and cholesterol. Garlic's healthful properties are most powerful when it is raw. Never burn garlic; it turns bitter.

Before they are dried, onions and garlic are called wet or fresh. By spring, they begin to sprout, lose flavour, and turn spongy. When cut, onions release a sulphurous compound that forms sulphuric acid in our eyes and makes us cry. But heat subdues the chemical, converting it into a substance fifty to seventy times sweeter than sugar. The lovely taste of browned onions results.

Onions are sensitive to day length and will not bulb in the wrong conditions. The cook as well as the farmer should know whether it is a long- or short-day type. Short-day onions are softer, milder, and do not store well. Long-day onions are hard, sharp, and keep well.

The yellow onion *Bedfordshire Champion* is an old English variety and an excellent keeper. White onions are generally smaller, and sweeter. Red or purple onions (*Sweet Sandwich* and *Long Red Florence*) are the sweetest.

The spring, salad, or green onion is a type of onion that is picked immature. Some, like *Ishikura*, are straight, with long white parts. Others form small bulbs.

The mild and subtle shallot is its own species of *allium*. Round or banana-shaped, it often has two or three cloves of pink or white flesh.

SEASON

Wet garlic: June and July. Dried garlic: July to March, when flavour and texture deteriorate. Spring onions: March to December. Shallots from August. Wet onions: from September. Dried onions: October to April, when they sprout and turn soft.

WHAT TO LOOK FOR

Firm, tight bulbs, heavy for their size. Garlic skin may be pink, purple, or white. No green sprouts.

STORAGE

In a cool, dry, dark place, away from other vegetables (the *allium* family hastens their spoilage). More pungent onions keep 2–3 months, red and other sweet onions 2–3 weeks. Spring onions last 3–4 days in the fridge.

MAKING THE MOST OF A SURPLUS

Red Onion and Pancetta Tart (p. 109), roasted garlic or onion soup.

PRAWNS IN GARLIC

I discovered this in the Canary Islands, where it turns up on every menu. It comes to the table in hot ceramic bowls with the sherry sizzling in the oil.

4–6 cloves garlic per person, peeled, and
   sliced in long strips
½–1 tsp dried chilli flakes per person
   (to taste)
1½ tbsp olive oil per person
8 raw prawns per person, peeled
2 tsp sherry per person
crusty bread

- Warm a bowl for each person in the oven.
- Heat the oil in a large frying pan and fry the garlic and chilli flakes over low heat until the garlic is half-cooked.
- Add the prawns and fry until they are almost cooked, stirring constantly. Add the sherry and turn up the heat until most of the alcohol has evaporated.
- Bring immediately to the table while it is still sizzling in the pan. Serve in hot bowls with bread to soak up the juices.

GRILLED POLENTA WITH GARLIC OIL

MAKES about 20 slices

2 large garlic cloves, smashed, peeled,
   and finely chopped
2 tbsp best olive oil
½ quantity Polenta (see p. 219)

- Cover the garlic with the olive oil.
- Slice the cooled polenta. Brush it on all sides with the garlic oil and grill or barbecue.

LOIN OF TUNA WITH BEETROOT & RED ONION CONFIT

Here the tuna is treated like a roast, with a spicy crust and rare centre. Don't worry if you do not have every spice: the essential flavours are cumin, cloves, and oregano.

SERVES 4

1 kg 'loin' of tuna

olive oil

red wine

For the marinade

2 tsp cumin seed (or 1½ tsp ground)

¼ tsp ground celery seed

¼ tsp ground oregano

4–5 cardamom seeds

6–10 whole cloves (or ½ tsp ground)

2 large cloves garlic, smashed, peeled, and finely chopped

¼ tsp salt

2 tbsp olive oil

For the confit

3 red onions, peeled and sliced

2 beetroots, grated

3 tbsp olive oil

1 large pear, peeled and sliced

200 ml red wine

1 tsp honey

¼ tsp salt

black pepper

- Toast the spices in a dry pan, but do not burn them.
- When they are cool, open the cardamom pods and discard the shells. Grind the spices with a mortar and pestle.
- Make a paste with the spices, garlic, salt, and olive oil.
- Rub the tuna on all sides with the marinade. Refrigerate for 4 hours or overnight.
- Make the confit. Sauté the onion and beetroot in the oil until they are soft.
- Add the pear, wine, honey, and salt. Simmer until the wine has reduced and the flavours are mellow, at least 20 minutes. Add black pepper to taste and set aside. This can be made the day before.
- In a heavy-bottomed saucepan just big enough for the fish, heat some olive oil. Brown the tuna on all sides, turning it gently to keep it intact. The oil should be hot, but not smoking.
- Splash some red wine over the tuna, cover the pan tightly, reduce the heat, and cook for 20–30 minutes until the fish is just pink in the centre, or well done if you prefer. Baste occasionally with a splash of wine and olive oil.
- Away from the heat, the fish continues to cook, so time it carefully or you will serve overdone tuna.
- Slice the fillets against the grain, pour the pan juices over it, and top it with the confit which you have rewarmed while the tuna was cooking.

ROAST CHICKEN WITH GARLIC SLICES & SAGE

The garlic gets completely mellow, suffusing the chicken with its fragrance.

SERVES 6

1.5–1.7 kg chicken
12 large cloves garlic, peeled and sliced
   longways, in flat discs
large handful fresh sage leaves, chopped
2 tbsp olive oil (you might use more)

- In the morning or at least 6 hours before eating, put the garlic and sage in the olive oil for at least 20 minutes.
- Coat your hands in the oil and slip them under the skin of the chicken, from both ends. Lay the garlic slivers flat and the sage leaves under the skin, spread evenly wherever you can reach. The garlic should make a pretty pattern of creamy ovals. Oil the chicken generously all over. Set it aside for the flavours to sink in.
- About 1½ hours before eating, set the oven to 200°C. Salt the chicken all over to make the skin crispy and roast, basting frequently with the olive oil and chicken juices. Salt again, if you like.
- Cook the chicken for about 25 minutes per kilogramme plus 20 minutes. Juices from the deep thigh should run clear when skewered.
- Allow it to rest outside the oven for 15 minutes before serving.
- For a quick clear gravy, sauté 1 finely chopped shallot in a saucepan, with juice from the roasting pan. When it is soft, add half a glass of white wine and cook until the alcohol has burned off.

> Why should roasted meats rest before eating? During cooking, juices are drawn out of the muscle. When it rests, they flow back into the meat, making it juicy.

RED ONION & PANCETTA TART

One for onion lovers. Bacon also works, as does red wine vinegar.

SERVES 6–8

200 g pancetta, cubed

1200 g red onions, about 6 large ones,
  peeled and sliced very thinly

3 tbsp butter

2 tbsp red wine

2 tbsp sherry vinegar

½ quantity Shortcrust Pastry (one crust),
  no sugar (see p. 218)

chives to garnish

- Brown the pancetta in a good-sized, heavy-bottomed saucepan.
- Add the onions and butter to the pan and cook until they are soft.
- Add the wine and the vinegar. Cook uncovered – so that the alcohol and vinegar evaporates – until the onions are soft, brown, and sweet, at least 45 minutes. Taste for salt and add more if necessary – but the pancetta is salty. (Cool, cover, and refrigerate for up to a day.)
- Set the oven to 180°C. Lay the pastry in a 25-cm tart tin. Warm the filling, then spread it evenly inside the pastry case. Bake until the crust is light brown, about 30 minutes.
- Top with chopped chives.

LENTILS WITH FRESH GARLIC

When wet or fresh garlic is cooked, it becomes mild very quickly, like elephant garlic. In winter, use dried garlic and chilli flakes, and eat with grilled sausages.

SERVES 2–4

1 large head fresh garlic, peeled and
  thickly sliced

1 red chilli pepper, seeded and
  finely chopped

2 bay leaves

2 tbsp olive oil

2–3 tbsp chopped chives

300 ml red wine

500 ml water

1 tsp salt

12 anchovies (optional)

200 g Puy lentils

- Sauté the garlic and chilli in the oil with the bay leaves. Do not allow to burn.
- When the garlic is soft, add the lentils and stir well to coat them with oil.
- Add the wine, water, and salt. Turn up the heat to burn off the alcohol. Stir and simmer until the lentils are soft, about 25 minutes. Remove the bay leaves.
- Rinse and drain the anchovies. Stir them into the lentils with the chives and serve warm.

PLE BUSH
BASIL

HERBS

Basil

Without herbs the cook would be lost. Not everyone has room or inclination to garden, but a few pots on a window-sill or in a porch make cooking with herbs easy and a pleasure.

Most culinary herbs come from the prolific mint and carrot families. The mints include basil, marjoram, thyme, oregano, rosemary, and sage. The strong flavour of the carrot family tends to be in its seeds, not leaves, giving us dill, fennel, anise, coriander, cumin, parsley, chervil, and caraway.

All the mints are Mediterranean natives, except basil, which is native to Asia and Africa. Basil comes in many flavours. *Sweet* or *Genovese* basil is the large-leafed classic used for pesto. *Purple Ruffles* and *Red Rubin* are pretty, but the purple basils have the least interesting flavour. Thai, cinnamon, and Greek basil are spicy, with smaller leaves. Lemon basil makes a fine vinaigrette for salads, asparagus, potatoes.

Use French or Italian flat parsley, which has a better flavour than curly. *Mitsuba* is Japanese parsley, and tastes like a cross between celery and parsley.

There are dozens of mints, from chocolate to orange to pineapple. Peppermint has the strongest flavour. Horseradish is a spicy root from the mustard family, best grated. Common green fennel and bronze fennel are the herbs related to the white bulb called Florentine fennel. They taste of aniseed. Chives are a miniature onion that grows in clumps, and garlic chives are flat. The purple flowers are nice in salads. Fresh coriander is indispensable in Mexican salsa and with Asian fish dishes.

The stronger winter herbs – rosemary, sage, oregano, winter savoury – must be finely chopped for cooking. They are wonderful with roasted vegetables and meats. Small new sage leaves in spring are lovely with new carrots and potatoes. Fry them whole.

If you have room for an easy-going bay tree, try fresh bay leaves, which taste springier than dried. Dried thyme, with bay and parsley, is a key ingredient of the French bouquet garni used in soups. The tiny leaves of lemon thyme are fiddly, but it really tastes of lemon.

SEASON

All year: perennials such as rosemary, bay, lavender, sorrel, winter savoury, sage, parsley, chives, fennel, lovage, peppermint, marjoram, thyme, tarragon. Spring to frost: chervil, angelica, caraway, fresh coriander, dill, summer savoury. Basil is a delicate summer herb, needing sun and heat.

WHAT TO LOOK FOR

Fresh green leaves. Stems freshly cut, not dry. Potted herbs in real soil are healthier plants than those grown in an artificial substitute.

STORAGE

In pots: water lightly and often. Keep on a window-sill and turn for even sun exposure. Cut: Do not wash, wrap in paper, and keep in a plastic bag in the fridge. Dried: Keep away from heat and light. Use quickly or buy in small quantities. They lose flavour like any other vegetable.

MAKING THE MOST OF A SURPLUS

Herb sugars, syrups, pastes, oils, and vinegars are easy to make with fresh herbs. To freeze, wash, dry, chop and put in plastic bags.

HERB SUGARS, SYRUPS & VINEGARS

Sugars

Any herb lends a delicate flavour to sugar. Put the chopped herbs in a small jar with the sugar and close the lid. Leave it overnight or a day or two in a cool, dry place. Try basil or lavender sugar on berries. Leave the berries in the sugar for at least 2 hours to draw out the juices. Biting a sugary leaf is delicious.

Syrups

Add chopped herbs or whole elderflowers to water and sugar, or to a poaching liquid. Refrigerate or freeze the syrup.

Flavoured vinegars

Put clean herbs, with stems (or raspberries or chillies) in a clean jar with good white wine vinegar. Close tightly and steep for a few days – or weeks or months. If the leaves or berries begin to look manky, strain it. You can also boil the vinegar with the herbs for 1–2 minutes.

Oils

Finely chop sturdy herbs like rosemary or mint and cover with olive oil. Strain or use as it is on pizzas, sauces, pastas, sandwiches, or for dressing vegetables. Whiz basil and oil for dipping bread.

HADDOCK WITH THAI BASIL & CHERRY TOMATO SALAD

Haddock is quite a bland-tasting fish; this recipe is meant to sharpen it up. Cinnamon basil is an acceptable substitute. Make the tomato salad first to allow the salt to draw out the juices.

1/2 punnet ripe cherry tomatoes per person
olive oil
1 haddock fillet per person

1 tsp chilli pepper flakes per person
1 bunch Thai basil per person

- Cut the tomatoes in half, and dress them lightly with olive oil, and salt to taste.
- In a food-processor or mortar and pestle, chop the basil leaves with 2 teaspoons of olive oil per person. (Or chop them finely on a cutting board, and mix with the oil.) The result should be like a rough pesto. Add salt to taste. Set aside.
- Heat 1 tablespoon of olive oil with 1 tsp chilli pepper flakes per person in a frying-pan. When the oil is hot and infused with chilli, sear the haddock fillets on each side for 1–2 minutes. Turn off the heat and cover the pan, allowing the centre of the fish to cook until it is ready, 4–5 minutes.
- Divide the pesto over the fish and eat hot with the tomato salad.

MUSSELS WITH PARSLEY & GARLIC

It is easy to vary the sauce: try basil, dill, finely chopped fennel, shallots, half of a fresh chilli or a teaspoon of flakes, 1 large leek, or about 25 ml of cream or passata. Mussels seeded on beds are not harvested during spawning from April to August. They are bigger and tastier than the rope-grown kind, which are available all year.

SERVES 2–4

2 kg mussels

4 cloves garlic, smashed, peeled,
  and finely chopped

50 ml olive oil

a glug of white wine

3 heaped tbsp parsley, chopped

- Keep live mussels for up to a day in a bucket of cold water in a cool pantry or in a bag in the fridge. Soak them in cold water for at least 20 minutes before cooking. They will release grit.
- Wash and scrub them in plenty of cold water, pulling off any stringy bits. Discard any open mussels; they are dead.
- About 10 minutes before eating, sauté the garlic with the olive oil in a large saucepan with a lid. Do not let it brown. Add the wine and the parsley and cook for 2 minutes. Season lightly.
- Add the mussels in one go, cover, shake the pot hard and let them steam for 5 minutes, until they open and release their juice. Stir or shake the pan and eat immediately.
- Serve the mussels from the pan into large soup bowls. Provide a large bowl for the shells, and plenty of bread to mop up the juice.

PRAWN PASTE WITH BASIL

This is based on an Elizabeth David recipe with dried basil. To de-vein prawns: peel the raw prawn, cut a narrow ditch down the spine and gently pull out the soft dark intestine.

SERVES 2

400 g raw prawns (about 200 g
  when cooked and peeled)

about 20 basil leaves

juice of $1/2$ lime

3 tbsp best olive oil

ground cayenne pepper (optional)

- Put the prawns in a smallish saucepan with a tight lid and let them steam in their own juice, like mussels, for about 10 minutes, until the flesh is firm and white.
- Strain them, reserving any strong red stock, peel.
- Process the prawns, stock, basil, lime juice, and olive oil until the paste is as smooth as you like it. Season with salt and cayenne to taste.

RABBIT MARINATED
IN ROSÉ & THYME

Rabbit is light and easy to cook. Do not skimp on the marinating time – or the thyme. Like most stews, it is better the day after it is cooked, which means that including the time needed for marinating, you will need to start 2 days before you plan to eat it.

SERVES 4–6

1.2 kg rabbit, cut in 8–10 pieces

4 tbsp olive oil for frying

1–2 tbsp plain flour

3 cloves garlic, smashed, peeled, and
finely chopped

1 shallot, finely chopped

10 sprigs thyme, leaves only

For the marinade

3 cloves garlic, smashed, unpeeled

1 shallot, sliced

1 bottle dry rosé

1 tbsp olive oil

1 tbsp pink peppercorns, crushed

2–3 fresh bay leaves

- The day before cooking, make the marinade. Pull off and chop a few thyme leaves. Tie the stalks in a bunch with string. Put the leaves, bunch of thyme, and all the other marinade ingredients in a large bowl with the rabbit and refrigerate for 12–24 hours.
- Remove the rabbit and pat it dry. Salt lightly.
- Heat 2 tablespoons of the olive oil in a heavy-bottomed pan large enough to hold all the rabbit. Do not let the oil smoke. Brown half the rabbit pieces, 5 minutes per side, and remove. Add more oil, if necessary, and then brown the rest.
- Put all the rabbit into the hot pan and pour in the marinade. Simmer until the rabbit is tender but still on the bone, about 1¼ hours.
- Turn off the heat and leave it to cool in the stock for up to 24 hours. (You can skip this step.)
- Remove the rabbit, bay leaves and bunched thyme from the stock. Strain a little stock and mix it with the flour until smooth.
- Sauté the garlic, shallot and thyme leaves in a little of the remaining oil.
- Purée the stock, freshly sautéed garlic mixture and stock-flour paste until smooth. Pour it into a saucepan and heat until the flour is cooked and the sauce has thickened. If there is too little sauce, thin it with water or wine. Put the rabbit back into the pan with the sauce and either heat it through and serve, or allow it all to cool and refrigerate until it is needed.
- Serve the rabbit and sauce over Soft Polenta (see p. 219).

CHERVIL SOUP

Chervil has a delicate flavour when cooked. My Belgian French teacher taught me this.

SERVES 2–4

100 g chervil leaves, chopped

extra chervil for stock

400 g waxy potatoes, peeled and diced,
    2 reserved for the stock

1 onion for stock

1 shallot or 2 spring onions, finely chopped

1 tbsp olive oil

2 tbsp best olive oil

- Make the chervil stock. Bring to the boil 1 litre of water with the chervil stems, the extra chervil, 1 potato, quartered and the onion, quartered. Cook for about 20 minutes, then strain.
- In a large saucepan, sweat the shallot or spring onions in the olive oil. Add the chervil stock and the diced potatoes and bring back to the boil, then reduce the heat to a simmer until the potaoes are half done. Add the chopped chervil leaves and simmer until the potatoes are soft but the chervil is still bright, about 5 minutes. Do not overcook.
- Stir in the best olive oil, check the salt, and serve.

CHICKEN SALAD WITH TARRAGON DRESSING

SERVES 4

1 shallot

½ bottle white wine

bay leaf

a large bunch of tarragon, for 2–3 tbsp
    chopped + extra sprigs

3 tbsp best olive oil

2 large chicken breasts, about 400 g,
    skinned

1 tbsp tarragon vinegar

1 heaping tbsp mayonnaise

1 tsp smooth Dijon mustard

fresh lemon juice

- Cut the shallot in half. Put it with the wine, bay leaf, 4–5 large whole sprigs of tarragon and the chicken in a saucepan. Add water to cover the chicken, if necessary and bring to the boil. Cover, turn off the heat, and poach for 15–20 minutes or until the chicken is done. Drain.
- While the chicken is poaching, finely chop the rest of the shallot and cover it with some of the olive oil. Leave it to stand – the longer it rests, the mellower it will be. Whisk the rest of the oil with the mayonnaise and mustard until it coheres. Add 2–3 tbsp chopped tarragon to taste, and transfer to a jar with the vinegar and the chopped tarragon. Shake it well, then season to taste.
- When the chicken is cool, separate the meat in to 4–6 cm long strips.
- Put the chicken into a bowl and toss it with the dressing. Squeeze over the lemon. Season to taste.
- Serve it alone or toss some watercress with olive oil and heap the chicken on top.

BEEF FILLET WITH A MUSTARD & ROSEMARY CRUST

Thanks to Margaret Ferrazzi for this one.

SERVES 4–6

2 heaped tbsp rosemary, leaves only

3 tbsp olive oil

1 large clove garlic, smashed and peeled

plenty of black pepper

5 tbsp grainy Dijon mustard

about 700 g beef fillet, trimmed

- Set the oven to 200°C.
- Whiz the rosemary, oil, garlic and pepper in a food-processor until smooth. Add the mustard and whiz again. It should be a thick, spreadable paste. Smear it on all sides of the beef, except the bottom, and bake for about 30 minutes. The paste should be dry and crispy.
- Rest the meat for 15 minutes then carve and serve warm. Delicious cold in sandwiches.

SALSA VERDE

An Italian green sauce with more flavours than pesto, salsa verde is not for overly sensitive palates. It is a classic accompaniment to monkfish and nice on anything you would dress with pesto: chicken, new potatoes, pasta. It should coat pasta thinly. The basic proportions are half parsley, quarter basil, quarter mint. Some people add a bit of Dijon mustard or red wine vinegar.

SERVES 8

large bunch parsley, leaves only

small bunch basil, leaves only

small bunch mint, leaves only

100 g capers, rinsed

100 g anchovies, rinsed

5 tbsp olive oil

3 cloves garlic, smashed and peeled

- Whiz everything in a food-processor until smooth. If you like more texture, keep back half of the herbs and add them at the end, pulsing briefly. Check the salt and grind in plenty of pepper.
- To coat 600 g pasta, thin the salsa verde with 1–2 tablespoons of the cooking water. The pasta should be slippery and glistening when it comes to the table.

LEEKS

I remember a cookbook called *First You Take a Leek*. Humour aside, it could describe my cooking. There's very little I wouldn't eat with the sweetest, mildest member of the *allium* family, which includes onions and garlic. You can begin to make any unplanned weekday meal by sautéing leeks. While they turn soft and sweet, you work out what else to cook. They make a delicious side dish cooked with sliced apples.

A large, perfect leek gives you 15 to 20 cm of thick white stalk. Buy more than you think you need; you discard a lot and they cook right down. To trim leeks, cut off the roots and remove the tough outer leaves, but keep the tender pale green centre. Cut them into rings or long strips.

It's essential to clean leeks properly. To keep them white, they are blanched – buried in soil up to the green part – so grit lies deep between the leaves. The easy way to wash leeks is by the salad leaf method (see p. 186) after chopping. Dunk them in plenty of cold water, swish the pieces around, and lift them out with your hands, letting water drip away before putting them in a colander, then repeating the exercise. The tougher green leaves are full of flavour, so add them to stocks.

If you want to braise or roast whole leeks, use smaller ones. In late summer, baby leeks are pretty served whole. They do not seem to let grit in, but neither do they have the deep sweetness of mature leeks.

Even a big leek can be tender if it has grown quickly, in good conditions, but an over-mature leek is woody. Don't boil any of the *alliums*: they get soggy and smell rotten. Braising is a good method for leeks. Brown them first, and then add a little water, stock or cream, and simmer. Unlike garlic and onions, leeks aren't nice raw.

SEASON

September to April.

WHAT TO LOOK FOR

Fresh roots, no yellow edges on the leaves, a bright white stalk.

STORAGE

Don't wash. Keep whole and dry in a plastic bag in the fridge. Use within 2–5 days.

MAKING THE MOST OF A SURPLUS

Sauté them all – they cook right down – and add to sandwiches and soups.

ROAST PHEASANT
WITH LEEK, SAGE &
OAT STUFFING

Pheasant dries out quickly. Do not overcook it. Baby leeks are around in the autumn.

SERVES 2

2 large cloves garlic

15 sage leaves

1 medium pheasant

10–12 baby leeks (pencil-sized) or 1 large
   leek, trimmed, washed and finely chopped

1 tbsp olive oil

100 g chopped porridge oats

1 egg

- Set the oven to 180°C.
- Sauté the garlic, sage, and leeks briefly in the oil to bring out the flavours.
- When the garlic is nearly done, mix in the oats and egg. You want roughly half oats and half leeks by volume. Season with salt and pepper.
- Rinse the pheasant and pat it dry inside and out. Rub it with olive oil inside and out. Stuff it and sprinkle the skin with salt and pepper.
- Roast the bird breast for up to 15 minutes, brush it with a little more oil, then roast it breast down for 15 minutes.
- Serve it with Butternut Purée (see p. 170)

JERUSALEM ARTICHOKE & LEEK SOUP

Do not peel Jerusalem artichokes, except for the odd rough bit. The skins are thin and full of iron. Earthy truffle oil and the quick Jerusalem artichoke stock are the secrets here. Leeks braised in Jerusalem artichoke stock are another delicious combination.

SERVES 4

For the stock

1 large leek, washed and trimmed

2–3 Jerusalem artichokes, scrubbed, chopped, unpeeled

1 tbsp olive oil

1.5 litres water

For the soup

3 tbsp olive oil

4 large leeks, washed, trimmed, and sliced

4 cloves garlic, smashed, peeled, and chopped

2 bay leaves

100 ml white wine

1 litre Jerusalem artichoke stock (see above)

1 kg Jerusalem artichokes, scrubbed and chopped

$1/2$ tsp salt

truffle oil

single cream to garnish (optional)

- To make the stock, heat the artichokes and leek in the olive oil, add water, and boil for 20 minutes, mashing vegetables a bit. Strain.
- In a large saucepan, sauté the leeks, garlic, and bay leaves in the olive oil until soft. Add the wine, raise the heat, and steam off.
- Add the artichokes, salt, and stock. Simmer until artichokes are soft, about 25 minutes.
- Strain off about 250 ml of stock and set aside. Remove the bay leaves, purée the rest until it is completely smooth, and season to taste.
- Stir in the remaining stock until you reach the desired thickness. Thick is homely, thin more elegant. If you like, stir in a spoonful of cream.
- Drizzle each bowl of soup with about 10 drops of truffle oil and serve hot with bread.

LEEKS À LA NIÇOISE

In summer, use ripe tomatoes, young leeks, and fresh thyme or summer savoury; in winter, tinned tomatoes, large leeks, and dried thyme. Black olives are a classic addition.

SERVES 2–4

1 kg leeks, trimmed and washed

1 tbsp thyme or summer savoury, chopped + some to garnish (or 1 tsp dried thyme)

400 g chopped tomatoes

3 cloves garlic, peeled, crushed, and finely chopped

2 tbsp olive oil

1 tbsp balsamic vinegar

2 tbsp red wine

- Slice mature leeks into rounds or, if small and very tender, in 4-cm lengths. Leeks are not easy to cut with a knife and fork, so cook them well if they are not bite-sized.
- Gently sauté the leeks in oil in a large, heavy frying-pan until they are translucent.
- Add half of the summer herbs or all of the dried herbs and all the other ingredients, including salt and pepper, cover, then simmer until the leeks are tender, adding a little water or tomato juice to keep them moist. In summer, top with the remaining herbs.
- Serve warm with plenty of juice and good bread to mop it up.

PAN-FRIED PORK FILLET WITH LEEKS & SAGE PESTO

SERVES 4

2 large handfuls sage leaves, no stems

4 tbsp olive oil + oil for searing pork

4 large leeks

1 large crisp eating apple such as *Cox*

4 pork fillets, fat trimmed

- In a blender, purée the sage with 2 tablespoons of the olive oil until smooth. If necessary, add a little water to catch the blades. Set a little of the pesto aside to drizzle over the pork.
- Cut the white part of the leeks in half longways, then again, making thin strips about 6 cm long. Rinse them in several changes of cold water.
- Sauté the leeks gently in the rest of the olive oil. After a few minutes, add the sage pesto and cook until the leeks are very soft and the raw sage flavour is gone. Slice the apple thinly and add it to the leeks. Stir, and cook until the apple slices are just soft but intact. Take the pan off the heat and keep warm.
- Brush the fillets with oil and season. Sear quickly on each side. Reduce heat and cook until white, about 10 minutes. Put a large spoonful of the leeks onto each plate, lay a piece of pork on top and drizzle with a little of the reserved sage pesto – it is quite strong.

MUSHROOMS

There are hundreds of species of mushroom, wild and cultivated. Most cultivated mushrooms are grown either in wood or in straw-based compost. Producers introduce mycelium, the mushroom's reproductive threads, into the growing medium.

Compost-grown mushrooms include the common or *button* mushroom or *champignon de Paris*. *Chestnut* is a brown button-type. *Portobello*, made fashionable by Californian restaurants, is a large, meaty common mushroom. Brown or white, it is often grilled and served whole. *Portobellos* have the best flavour two or three days after picking.

Mushrooms grown on logs or sawdust blocks are also picked all year, but they need an even temperature, so in either hot or cold weather there may be a shortage. The mushrooms grow indoors with carefully controlled light (including wave-length), temperature and moisture. Mushroom growing is all about trade secrets.

The delicate *oyster* mushroom is one of dozens of log-grown species. They come in all sizes and shapes, some with small blue-grey caps and others with oval, velvety brown ones. The flavour ranges from peppery to sweet to buttery.

Other log-grown species are *Hon Shimeji*, *Grifola*, *shiitake*, and *Beefsteak*. *Grifola*, or *Hen of the Woods*, forms a rosette of overlapping layers and tastes a bit like chicken. The Asian *shiitake* is brown and flat with a tough stem, and has a strong, meaty flavour. *Shiitake* are often sold dried; one goes a long way. *Beefsteak* is flat and red. It looks like an ox-tongue and tastes slightly sharp, like sorrel. When cut, it bleeds a red juice, which makes a dark sauce when cooked.

Many wild mushrooms grow in a symbiotic relationship with a tree. The fungus extracts sugars from the tree roots, and the tree takes up phosphorous from the mushroom. *Penny Bun* is the English name for *porcini* and *cèpes*, which grow under beeches. Another species, *Chanterelle*, grows near conifers. *Puffballs* and *field* mushrooms are also gathered from the wild.

SEASON

Button and *oyster* mushrooms: all year. *Puffballs*: mid- to late summer.
Chanterelles: summer. *Cèpes* or *porcini*: late summer, early autumn.
Beefsteak: spring and autumn.

WHAT TO LOOK FOR

Firm, unbruised. Dry, not slimy, with unbroken gills. Clean, unscratched skin, the cut end of the stalk still fresh. *Button* mushrooms: gills go from pink when freshly picked to brown to black.

STORAGE

Refrigerate in perforated plastic or paper bag. *Oyster* and *button* mushrooms last about a week, *shiitake* longer.

MAKING THE MOST OF A SURPLUS

Mushroom stock is easy, quick, and useful (see p.128).

MUSHROOM STEW WITH CROSTINI

*In Islington, just down the street from London's first farmers' market, is the **Duke of Cambridge**, the city's first all-organic gastro-pub. Organic farmers at the market also supply the restaurant. (See Sea Bass Baked in Fennel & Pernod, p. 100.)*

SERVES 4

20 g dried *porcini* or *cèpe* mushrooms

½ yellow onion, peeled and chopped

2 large cloves garlic, smashed, peeled, and chopped

1 tsp fresh thyme, chopped

1 tsp fresh rosemary, chopped

1 tsp fresh sage, chopped

3 tbsp olive oil

500 g potatoes, peeled and sliced

1 glug sherry

200 g fresh field, *oyster*, or *shiitake* mushrooms, wiped and sliced

½ tsp salt

500 ml vegetable (see p.129) or mushroom stock (see below)

black pepper

Parmesan (optional)

For crostini

1 loaf crusty country bread

2 large cloves garlic, peeled and sliced in half

best olive oil

- Soak the porcini in 300 ml water for about 30 minutes.
- Sauté the onion, garlic, and herbs in olive oil.
- Drain and squeeze the dried mushrooms, reserving the soaking liquid, and add to the pan. Fry hard, stirring constantly. Add the potatoes and continue to fry. After a minute add the fresh mushrooms and fry until they release their juice.
- Strain the mushroom water through a muslin cloth.
- Add a glug of sherry to the pan with the mushroom water and boil it for a minute or two.
- Add the salt and stock. Cover and simmer until the potatoes are cooked, 10–15 minutes. Grind in some black pepper and check the salt.
- Toast thick slices of country bread. Rub one side with the cut side of a large garlic clove and drizzle or brush with best olive oil.
- Pour the soup into the bowls and top each with a crostini. Sprinkle over some Parmesan if you like.

> Mushroom stock is handy for rice, soup, even pasta, and is not a bad way in which to use mushrooms just past their prime: sauté mushrooms, garlic, and a bay leaf in a bit of olive oil; add 1 litre of water and simmer until the mushrooms have given up their flavour. Keeps for a week in the fridge.

RISOTTO WITH OYSTER MUSHROOMS

SERVES 2–4

1 litre mushroom or chicken stock

1 medium yellow onion, finely chopped

3 large cloves garlic, smashed, peeled, and finely chopped

3 tbsp olive oil

300 g Arborio or other short-grain rice

500 g *oyster* mushrooms, wiped and chopped

¼–½ tsp salt, depending on stock

4 tbsp freshly grated good Parmesan

1 tbsp chopped parsley

- Make a quick mushroom stock (opposite) or use 2 mushroom-flavoured stock cubes.
- In a large, heavy pan, sauté the onion and garlic in the oil until soft. Add the mushrooms and fry until they release their juice, 3–4 minutes. Add the rice and stir to coat it with the oil.
- Add the stock gradually in small amounts, stirring constantly as it's absorbed, about 20 minutes. When the rice is cooked to your taste and the sauce is creamy, check the seasoning. Beware oversalting. Stir in the cheese and sprinkle with parsley.

TAGLIATELLE WITH SHIITAKE MUSHROOMS

SERVES 4

100 g dried *shiitake* mushrooms

1 clove garlic, finely chopped

2 shallots, finely chopped

1 fresh bay leaf

about 20 6-cm sprigs lemon thyme

2 tbsp olive oil

100 g fresh *shiitake* and *oyster* mushrooms, wiped and chopped

about 140 ml single cream

1 tbsp sherry

good Parmesan for grating

300 g tagliatelle

squeeze lemon juice (optional)

- Soak the shiitake in 500 ml water for 20–30 minutes. Remove the shiitake from the water and squeeze gently. Strain the water through muslin and reserve. Slice the mushrooms.
- Put the dried shiitake and thyme stems into a large saucepan with plenty of salted water and a little olive oil. Boil it hard for about 5 minutes, then skim out the aromatics.
- Sauté shallots, garlic, bay leaf and thyme in a large frying pan with the olive oil for 2–3 minutes, then add the dried and fresh mushrooms. When the mushrooms are nearly soft, add half of the mushroom soaking liquid, cream, and sherry. Taste and season. Continue to simmer.
- Bring the scented water back to the boil and put in the tagliatelle.
- When the mushrooms are soft most of the liquid will have been absorbed. At the last minute, stir in the cheese, and lemon juice. Drain the pasta and toss it with the sauce. Serve immediately.

PARSNIPS

The parsnip is a taproot in the carrot family. A poisonous cousin grows wild in Eurasia, but the sweet parsnip we know is a Mediterranean vegetable which was familiar to the Greeks and Romans. Parsnips were an important staple all over Europe before that conquering starch, the potato, arrived from the New World. Sadly the colonists did not eat the parsnip with the same enthusiasm, and it is still under-appreciated in America, although in Jamestown, in the early seventeenth century, the settlers made a wedding cake with parsnip flour.

Parsnips are first dug in late September, then stored in root cellars. They can also be left in the ground, where they keep well until February or March. They are sweeter after a light frost, which converts some of the starch to sugar.

A tender parsnip is 5–6 cm across. Large roots have a tough core and woody texture. *Tender and True*, a Victorian variety with a long root, and *White Gem*, a shorter one, have the best flavour. Parsnips are rich in potassium, folic acid, and vitamin B6.

Do not peel parsnips. The skin is thin, and positively delicious when roasted. Try not to boil them either, unless you are making purée or glazed parsnips. They get soggy in water. They are better roasted or sautéed, which removes water and concentrates the sugars. Sautéing takes patience and the parsnips must be cut into small pieces. Parsnips are good glazed. Put them in a wide, shallow pan with butter, honey, salt, and just enough water to cover them – or apple juice, if you have a sweet tooth. Cover the pan and bring it to the boil, then remove the lid and reduce until the liquid is dark and thick. Parsnips go well with nutmeg, cream, Jerusalem artichokes, and leeks.

As with all vegetables, the trick to perfect doneness lies in cutting the parsnips into even pieces. My method: cut the root in thirds cross-wise, so you have a thin, medium, and thick piece. Set each piece on its end, like a stump, and cut downward, in sticks of equal thickness. You will get more sticks from the thick piece, and just a couple from the thin end, but they will all be the same size.

SEASON

Dug in late September, early October. From storage (or the ground) until March.

WHAT TO LOOK FOR

Firm, heavy for their size. An old parsnip is light and spongy. Uneven skin is fine, but avoid spots of rot.

STORAGE

In the fridge or as cool as 0°C for several weeks. Or let the farmer store them!

MAKING THE MOST OF A SURPLUS

Purée is convenient and freezes well.

STEWED SHOULDER OF LAMB
WITH PARSNIPS & PEARS

The shoulder is the sweetest cut. Here it is stewed until it is falling off the bone with sweet flavours: pink peppercorns, parsnips, and pears. Fresh bay leaves right off the plant are more pungent than dried.

SERVES 6–8

1 shoulder of lamb, about 2 kg

75 ml olive oil for braising

4 large leeks, trimmed, washed and sliced

4 fresh bay leaves

1 tbsp pink peppercorns, crushed

250 ml rosé

250 ml lamb or vegetable stock

500 g parsnips

2 firm pears, such as *Concord*

- Heat half of the olive oil in a large, heavy saucepan with a tight lid. Brown the lamb well, about 5–7 minutes on each side. Do not let the oil smoke or the meat burn.
- Remove the lamb from the pan, discard the fat, wipe the pan, then heat the remaining olive oil gently.
- Add the leeks, bay leaves, and pink peppercorns. When the leeks begin to soften, add the wine and stock.
- Set the lamb on top of the leeks, baste, and cover. Cook for at least 3 and probably 4 hours on the lowest heat, until the meat is very tender. If the lid is not tight-fitting, weigh it down. Baste once or twice during the cooking time but don't leave the lid off: the lamb is partly poaching, partly steaming. A low oven or slow-cooker also works well.
- About an hour before the lamb is finished, wash and cut the parsnips and pears in bite-sized pieces. Do not peel.
- Add parsnips and pears, turn the meat, and cook until parsnips are soft.
- Check for salt and add more pink pepper to taste.
- Carve the lamb, and serve it with a few spoonfuls of vegetables and some stock, in a bowl on its own or over rice.

> This is even tastier the next day. After seasoning, store it in a cool pantry or the fridge. Lamb is rich: when the fat has risen and congealed, lift it out and discard it. Reheat and serve.

SMOKED HADDOCK & PARSNIP FISHCAKES

If you do not use smoked fish, add 1 tsp anchovy essence or fish sauce before forming the cakes. Or salt to taste.

MAKES 8–10 cakes

450 g parsnips, peeled and chopped

25 g butter

400 g un-dyed smoked haddock

350 ml milk

1 tsp turmeric

1–2 eggs

2 tbsp chives, chopped

mixture of flour and fine polenta for dusting

vegetable or light olive oil for frying

Aïoli to garnish (see p. 218)

- Boil the parsnips in salted water. Drain and mash lightly, mixing in the butter.
- Heat the haddock in the milk and turmeric until simmering point, then remove from heat and drain. Remove the skin and flake the fish.
- Beat 1 egg and mix it with the fish, chives, and plenty of fresh black pepper.
- Gently mix the parsnips and fish. Flour your hands and form cakes about 2 cm thick and 6–7 cm across. They can be refrigerated for several hours.
- If the fishcakes are moist, pat them on all sides with the flour and polenta. If they are dry, brush them with the second beaten egg, and then dust them with the flour and polenta.
- Heat enough oil in a heavy pan to brown the fishcakes half-way up each side. Fry each side for 3–4 minutes, until crisp. Drain on kitchen paper and serve hot with Aïoli.

Variation: Mix 1 tsp each of ground cayenne and turmeric into the flour and polenta mixture.

ROASTED PARSNIPS WITH HONEY

Roasted vegetables are easy and delectable. Try any simple combination of carrots, parsnips, swede, beetroot, potatoes, or winter squash, cut into cubes or fat matchsticks, with a fresh herb.

SERVES 2–4

500 g parsnips (about 3 large), cut
  as discussed on p. 131

2 shallots, finely chopped

2 tsp olive oil

freshly grated nutmeg

1 tsp honey

- Set the oven to 220°C.
- Mix the parsnips and shallots together with the olive oil in a baking tin. Sprinkle some salt and grate fresh nutmeg over them.
- Spread them evenly in not more than two layers and bake until the edges are brown and they begin to stick, about 10 minutes. Set the timer, or you may burn them.
- Shake the pan, stir in the honey, reduce the heat to 180°C, and cook until tender, about 15–20 minutes. Shake the pan occasionally to prevent sticking.

PARSNIP PURÉE

SERVES 2–4

800 g parsnips, chopped

200 g potatoes, peeled and chopped

1 large yellow onion, chopped

½ tsp salt

1 sprig rosemary, leaves chopped roughly

2 bay leaves

2 tsp olive oil

- Put all the ingredients except the oil into a saucepan with some water, bring it to the boil and cook until vegetables are soft. Drain, reserving a little water.
- Purée with the oil, thinning to taste with the reserved cooking water. Season with salt and pepper.

Variations: Cook a *Bramley* apple, peeled and quartered, with the parsnips and potatoes.

PEARS

Farmers' markets spur growers to outdo their fellow stall-holders, dazzling customers with more varieties, every one with more spectacular flavour, texture, or colour than the next. This competition delights cooks; it also has a healthy effect on biodiversity. Here, again, is the wonderful Raymond Bush, in *Tree Fruit Growing*, vol. II: 'John Scott, a famous Somersetshire nurseryman around 1870, had a collection of eighteen hundred different varieties of pear. Today his firm lists no more than thirty-six.' Bush was lamenting lost varieties in 1943. Now just *three* varieties account for 94 per cent of Britain's pear orchards. Between 1970 and 1996, almost half the nation's pear orchards disappeared, some of them grubbed up with European Union grants.

The common mistake of the amateur grower is letting pears ripen on the tree, which makes them mealy and grainy. The pear's smooth, creamy texture depends on being picked under-ripe. Early and mid-season varieties such as *Williams Bon Chrétien* (often plain *Williams*) may show a bit of brownish red, but the base colour must be green, without a yellow tint, for proper ripening off the tree. Mid-season pears such as *Conference* are also picked with a green base beneath their russeting. In storage, the green changes to yellow, pink, and red, although some pears, such as the French *Anjou*, are still green when ready to eat. Storage is quite cool, 6–10°C. At home, the pear's full flavour will develop at room temperature, about 12°C.

The most common British pear is the creamy *Conference*. Its name comes from winning first prize at the International Pear Conference in London in 1885. It is long and smooth, with smooth sweet flesh, and often no pips at all. The stubby *Williams* (*Bartlett* in America) is aromatic and excellent for poaching as well as eating. There's also *Red Williams*. *Comice* is French, and often eaten with cheese. Squat, with a short neck, it is golden when ripe and exceptionally sweet. *Concord* is yellow, with crispy, almost apple-like flesh, and keeps well.

The main clue to pear ripeness is colour. Most pears show a faint yellow background when ready. *Anjou* and other green ones should give slightly under pressure. Once ripe, the pear's flavour deteriorates quickly.

SEASON

Early pears: from August. Main crop: September and October. Excellent fruit from storage until March, quality waning in April and May.

WHAT TO LOOK FOR
Smooth skin, no cuts. Russeting is fine. Firm, heavy for their size.

STORAGE

To keep, store loose at 6–10°C. Ripen at room temperature. To speed ripening, put pears in a paper bag with other ripe fruit such as a banana to trap the ethylene gas.

MAKING THE MOST OF A SURPLUS

Smoothies are good for soft fruit, as long as it does not taste overripe. Delicious with milk or yoghurt, nutmeg, and almonds.

PEAR SMOOTHIES

Creamy pears make great smoothies. You only need a blender. You get all the nutrients and fibre and they only take a minute. These recipes make one large or two small glasses.

APPLE, PEAR & GINGER

200 ml apple juice

1 ripe pear, unpeeled

1-cm piece of ginger, unpeeled

• Quarter the pear and remove the pips. Blend everything until smooth.

GRAPE, PEAR & GINGER

500 g grapes

1 ripe pear, unpeeled

1-cm chunk ginger, unpeeled

• Follow the instructions for Apple, Pear & Ginger

PEAR, NUTMEG & HONEY

1 large ripe pear, unpeeled

1 tsp honey

300 ml milk or yoghurt

freshly grated nutmeg

• Follow the instructions for Apple, Pear & Ginger

PEAR TREAT

I did not know what to call this, but it is a delicious dessert or snack for one.

1 pear, diced

1 tbsp pine kernels, toasted

1 tsp best olive oil

1 tsp honey

• Mix together all the ingredients thoroughly and eat immediately.

WATERCRESS, PEAR & GOAT'S CHEESE SALAD

Sweet pear, sharp cress, mild creamy cheese.

SERVES 2–4

100 g watercress, chopped,
   bigger stems removed

2 firm pears such as *Conference*,
   cored and diced

50 g young goat's cheese

1 tbsp chives, chopped

3 tbsp apple juice

3 tbsp best olive oil

- Put the juice and the oil into a jar and shake well.
- Mix together the pears and cress. Crumble the cheese over them.
- Dress the salad and season.

PEARS POACHED IN RED WINE
WITH CANDIED PEEL & ALMONDS

In most fruit and vegetables, nutrients and flavour lurk just beneath the skin, so it is a shame to peel them. I always poach pears with the peel. Poaching is a good way to use slightly underripe fruit. Almonds with pears is a Spanish combination.

SERVES 6

6 firm, ripe pears, *Conference* or *Concord*	1 vanilla pod
1 bottle red wine	freshly grated nutmeg
6 whole cloves	1 knob butter
6 black peppercorns	3 tbsp whole almonds, peeled
100 g sugar	

- Slice the bottoms of the pears flat and peel them, leaving a little flesh on the peel, and the stem on the pear.
- Put all the ingredients except the butter and the almonds into a saucepan and simmer until the pears are cooked, about 25 minutes depending on ripeness. They should still be firm.
- Remove the pears with a slotted spoon and set them aside. Simmer the liquid until it is reduced by half. You can make this dish a day in advance: if so, pour the syrup over the pears so that they stay moist, reserving about 2 tablespoons.
- Remove most of the peel from the syrup, taking care not to pick up any peppercorns or cloves.
- Heat the reserved syrup, the butter, and the almonds in a clean pan. Simmer until the sugar has caramelised, not more than 8 minutes. Do not let it burn.
- Place each pear in a bowl, pour some syrup over it, and top it with a spoonful of almonds and peel. It will be a sticky mess, and will stiffen slightly as it cools.
- Serve with Custard (see p. 218)

Variation: Poach pears with herbs and white wine for a different spicy flavour. Add 4–5 tbsp chopped rosemary or basil, including the stems.

PEAS

Once Europeans ate peas only when they were dried in porridge. Fresh, immature peas were an innovation at the court of Louis XIV. They are still a luxury. In good company, shelling garden peas is fun and worth the effort. As good as frozen peas are, fresh ones are unsurpassed. The mangetout promises pea flavour for very little work. Just trim the flat green pods, steam them and dress them with olive oil. But they are neither as sweet nor as flavourful as a garden pea. The best of both worlds is the sugar snap, a cross between shelled peas and mangetout. It has good-sized peas, and the pod is fleshy, tender, plump, and sweet. Trim the ends, pull off the string, and eat the whole, plump thing.

Like sweetcorn, peas convert their sugars to starch from the moment they are picked and should be eaten as soon as possible. The grower should keep them cool and shaded, the basket lined in wet cloth or paper even at market. Maturity is as important to flavour as freshness, and trickier: careful pickers know a perfect garden pea by sight. Too old, and the peas are square and starchy. Too young, and the flavour is bland, the peas too small. At market, the customer should try to avoid pods that are too fat, slightly square, whitish, or wrinkly. Taste one.

Garden peas come in two kinds, smooth and wrinkly. The smooth ones are winter hardy and come in early; wrinkly ones are later and sweeter. *Greenshaft, Kelveden Wonder,* and *Lincoln* are wrinkly ones prized for flavour. *Oregon Sugar Pod* and *Crouby de Maussanne* are mangetout with excellent flavour. *Sugar Rae* is a good sugar snap.

Compared with most green vegetables, the garden pea is rich in protein – 25 per cent. Cooked, all three fresh peas are a good source of folic acid, potassium, iron, and vitamins C and B6. To preserve flavour, colour, and nutrients, fresh peas should be cooked briefly. Steam or stir-fry them, and remove them from the heat immediately to stop the cooking. Add shelled peas at the last minute to soups and risotto. You might blanch mangetout for a moment before adding them to salads. Sugar snaps are delicious raw.

SEASON

Mangetout: June to August. Shelled peas: June to August. Sugar snaps: July and August.

WHAT TO LOOK FOR

Bright green, intact pods, no wrinkles. Over-mature or old garden peas have whitish, striated pods.

STORAGE

Keep cool in transit. Refrigerate in a bag as soon as possible. Eat within 1–2 days.

MAKING THE MOST OF A SURPLUS

Why freeze garden peas when commercial ones are so good? But local sugar snaps and mangetout are worth freezing. Trim, blanch for 1 minute in salted water, dry, and freeze.

PEA & FENNEL PURÉE

For a brief time at the end of the pea season, there is new fennel, and they are wonderful together. Delicious with roast chicken or spread on toast.

SERVES 2–4

1 large fennel bulb

1 tbsp olive oil

10 mint leaves

600 g peas, shelled

2 tbsp best olive oil

- Sauté the fennel gently in the olive oil until it is soft, about 20 minutes.
- Boil just enough salted water to cover the . Add the peas. When the water boils again, they are almost done. Peas should be bright green and tender. Drain them and keep the cooking water.
- Purée the peas with the fennel, mint, and 1½ tablespoons of the best olive oil. Add 4–6 tablespoons of the pea water and more best olive oil until you reach the consistency you like. Season to taste.

PEA MEDLEY WITH MINT PESTO

Use new-growth mint. The old leaves are tough.

SERVES 2–4

3 tbsp roughly chopped mint leaves

juice of 1 orange

2 tbsp best olive oil

300 g mixed peas (mangetout, shelled peas, sugar snaps)

- Blend the mint and the oil in a mortar and pestle or in a blender.
- Boil the peas in salted water until crisp-tender, 5–6 minutes. Drain and then remove from the hot pan, lest they overcook.
- Toss with the mint, the pesto, orange juice, and season with salt and pepper. Eat immediately, before the mint goes brown.

Variation: Use mint oil instead of pesto. Mint keeps in a plastic bag in the fridge longer than most herbs, but if it is about to go brown, chop it and cover it with olive oil. It keeps for up to 2 weeks. Use as it is, or strain it.

BAKED OMELETTE WITH PEAS & HOT SMOKED TROUT

Frozen peas work fine, without defrosting.

SERVES 4–6

200 g hot-smoked trout

8 eggs

150 ml milk

1/2 tsp salt

3 tbsp chives, finely chopped

olive oil

300 g peas, shelled

- Set the oven to 180°C. Flake the trout with a fork. Whisk the eggs with the milk, salt, chives, and plenty of black pepper.
- Oil a large ovenproof frying-pan. Add the trout and peas to the eggs and pour it into the pan, stirring so that the peas and trout are not clumped together.
- Put the pan into the oven and bake until the omelette is set but creamy in the middle, about 20 minutes. The peas should be bright green and pop when you bite them. Eat warm or cold with a green salad or Gazpacho (see p. 216).

Variation: Try spring onions instead of chives, asparagus instead of peas. Cut the asparagus into 2-cm pieces and blanch for 1 minute before adding it to the eggs. Save tips and arrange them on top when the omelette is half set.

PAELLA

Paella pans are shallow and ovenproof. Serve paella in the pan. The bottom should be crusty, and the rice dryer than risotto.

SERVES 4–6

200 g squid, untrimmed
1 medium lobster, cooked
6 large prawns
10 mussels, cleaned
200 g white fish, or chicken fillet,
    sausage or rabbit

For the rice
10 cloves garlic, smashed, peeled, and
    finely chopped
about 30 ml olive oil
400 g short-grained rice such as Arborio
1½ tsp paprika

6 tbsp parsley, finely chopped
100 ml Passata (see p. 215)
300 g peas, shelled

For the stock
1 bay leaf
1 tsp saffron threads
1 clove garlic, smashed and peeled
1 tsp olive oil
100 ml white wine
fish shells and bones

1 quantity Aïoli to garnish (see p. 218)

- To make stock, separate the squid body from the innards. Refrigerate the body and put the scraps into a large saucepan. Crack the lobster claws and cut the tail into pieces. Cover and refrigerate the claws and the tail. Put the lobster body in the saucepan.
- Cook the prawns gently in a covered pan until the flesh is firm and white, about 5 minutes. Refrigerate the prawns. Cut the fish into bite-sized pieces and the squid into rings. Refrigerate.
- Add garlic, wine, saffron, and oil to the fish scraps, and sauté until the oil coats fish and the wine steams. Add 1½ litres of water to the pan and simmer for 20 minutes. Scrub the mussels and soak in cold water for at least 30 minutes. While the stock is simmering, steam mussels in a covered pan until they open. Add the mussel liquor to the stock. Strain, add salt to taste and set aside.
- About 40 minutes before serving, bring the stock to the boil. Set the oven to 190°C.
- In the paella pan lightly brown the fish and squid in batches with fresh oil each time. Set aside.
- Add the rice to the boiling stock, reduce the heat and simmer for 5-8 minutes.
- Sauté the garlic, paprika, and half of the parsley in olive oil until the garlic is soft. Add the passata. Mix well, then add the half-cooked rice, with any unabsorbed stock.
- Mix the fish, peas and squid, but not the shellfish, into the rice. Cook for 10 minutes or less, adding a bit of extra hot stock if the rice is dry. Check seasoning.
- Arrange the prawns, mussels, and lobster claws in a circular pattern and bake for 10 minutes, or until the rice is *al dente*.
- Remove from the heat and rest for 10 minutes. Serve with Aioli, parsley, and a squeeze of lemon.

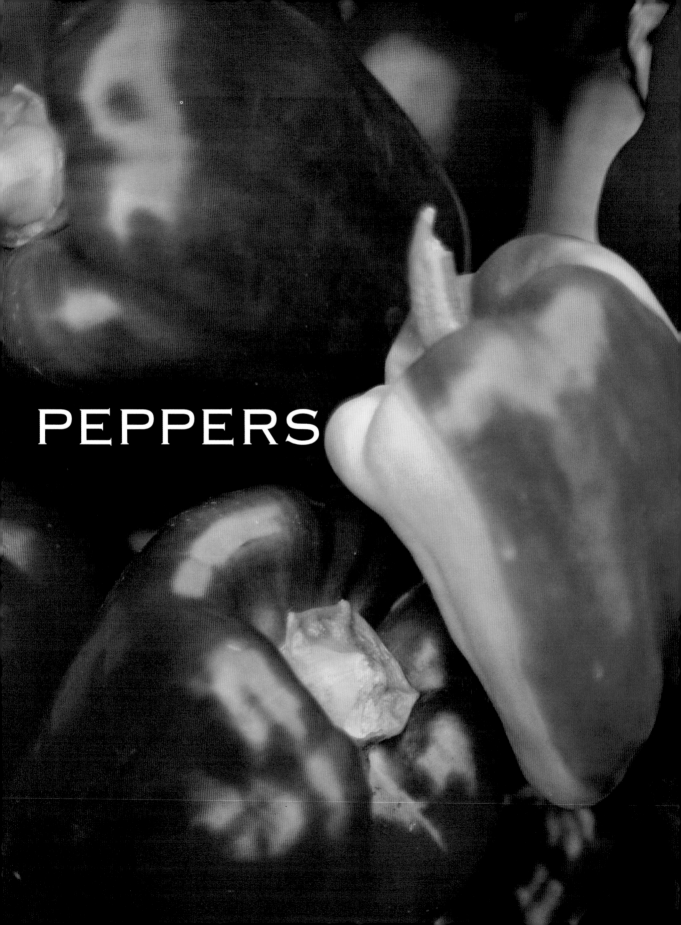

PEPPERS

Every green pepper on our farm is allowed to ripen to red, orange, or yellow.

In other words the green and red bell pepper are the same vegetable at different stages of ripeness. Red, orange, and yellow peppers are fully ripe and sweet. Green, chartreuse, chocolate, blue, and purple peppers are underripe. They will eventually turn a bright colour and become sweeter if left on the plant. Like its fellow nightshade, the tomato, the pepper begins to ripen once it reaches full size.

As the pepper ripens, it makes more sugar, more vitamin A and C, and more beta-carotene. Unlike the tomato or pear, its flesh does not soften, but the aroma and flavour improve markedly. A pepper that has begun to ripen on the plant will ripen fully after picking. Keep it at room temperature out of the sun. *Eagle* (orange) and *Beauty Bell* (red) have good flavour.

Lovely as bell peppers are, we were bowled over when we discovered the stronger flavour of sweet Italian frying peppers. Try these pointed, thin-fleshed peppers in any sauté or salad. *Long Red Marconi* and *Long Yellow Ringo* are good varieties.

The chilli is the most-consumed spice in the world. The sting of capsaicin in chillies prompts the body to release a wave of painkilling endorphins, a natural opiate that turns up in other nice circumstances – like sex. The best antidote to chillies is milk or starch. Alcohol merely increases the absorption of capsaicin.

Aficionados taste many flavours, from citrus to tobacco, but most of us know chillies as mild, hot or scorching. The Scoville heat rating is helpful. The sweet bell pepper rates a 0, while the fearsome *Habanero*, the hottest pepper in the world, earns a 10. *Cayenne, Serrano,* and *Jalapeño*, three common chillies, are in the lower middle range. *Hungarian Wax* is a mild pepper that turns slightly hot as it ripens. Generally, the smaller the pepper, the hotter it is. Capsaicin increases with ripeness, so a green cayenne is milder than a red one.

It is easy to control chilli heat in the kitchen. Much of the heat is in the pinkish-white fibres holding the seeds. For a hotter dish, chop the whole chilli; for a milder one, use only the flesh. Cooking also subdues chillies.

SEASON

July to November, often under glass; chillies can grow indoors all year.

WHAT TO LOOK FOR

Bell peppers: firm, shiny and heavy for their size. Chillies: unblemished and taut, not shrivelled or wrinkly. Like tomatoes, half-red peppers ripen beautifully at room temperature.

STORAGE

To ripen, keep at room temperature, out of the sun. They do not need chilling, but the refrigerator won't harm ripe peppers.

MAKING THE MOST OF A SURPLUS

Roasted red peppers keep well. Frozen sweet and chilli peppers are fine for winter sauces. Slice, blanch in boiling salted water, and freeze in bags. Finely chop but do not blanch chillies.

LOBSTER & RED PEPPER SALAD

SERVES 2

100 g watercress, untrimmed weight

2 tbsp tarragon, finely chopped

1 tbsp tarragon vinegar or
  fresh lemon juice

2 tbsp best olive oil

¼ tsp smooth Dijon mustard

1 red or yellow bell pepper,
  cut in very thin strips

200 g lobster meat

ground cayenne (optional)

- Trim the watercress stems; chop any large leaves.
- Mix tarragon vinegar, oil, and mustard in a jar and shake well. It benefits from resting an hour or more. Toss the watercress and the peppers in one bowl and the lobster in another; the dressing coats better that way. Season to taste.
- Mound the lobster on a bed of salad, or mix both together.

ROASTED SWEET PEPPERS

These keep for a week in the fridge and go with anything. The ratio is roughly 1 pepper to 2 cloves of garlic to 1 teaspoon of oil.

1.5 kg large red, yellow, or orange peppers
  cut in long slices about 2 cm wide

10–12 large cloves garlic, peeled and cut
  in thick slices

50 ml olive oil

- Set the oven to 180°C. Toss everything well with oil and salt. Roast in not more than 2–3 layers for about 45 minutes, shaking occasionally. They should be meltingly tender not crispy.
- Eat warm or cold, on their own or on toast, pizza, polenta, in sandwiches and salads. If you want to keep them for longer, put them into a jar with some olive oil. Roasted peppers, pesto, and toasted pine kernels make a lovely salad.

FAJITAS WITH ITALIAN FRYING PEPPERS & SALSA

You will never see fajitas in Mexico: they are Tex-Mex, invented by border workers who had some tough meat, and so they marinated it. Ask the butcher to cut the skirt steak in one long flat strip and trim the fat. One person eats 3 small (15 cm) or 2 large (22 cm) flour tortillas. The secret is not to overfill them.

SERVES 4–6

600 g skirt steak

2 large cloves garlic, peeled and chopped

75 ml olive oil + extra for sautéing

3–4 limes (or orange juice)

1 long red Italian frying pepper

1 long yellow Italian frying pepper

1 medium red onion

flour tortillas

fresh coriander to garnish

For the spice rub

2 tbsp California chilli powder

2 tbsp pasilla chilli powder

1 tbsp ancho chilli powder

2 tbsp paprika

2 tbsp ground cumin

1 tsp ground oregano

or: 7 tbsp all-purpose chilli powder

  + paprika and oregano

For the salsa

2 quantities of Classic Salsa Cruda (see p. 211)

- The day before: mix spices and rub them over the meat on all sides. Refrigerate overnight.
- At least two hours before: mix the garlic with the olive oil and lime juice and marinate the meat, turning it once or twice.
- When you're ready to cook: slice the peppers and the onion into long strips, thinner than a pencil.
- Make the salsa – any earlier and it gets watery.
- Heat a ridged grill pan or barbecue very hot. Drain the meat and grill it until it is well browned but just pink in the centre. It will cook a bit more on the plate.
- Wrap the tortillas in foil and warm them in the oven. While the meat is grilling, sauté the peppers and onions in olive oil until soft. Keep them warm.
- Cut the meat into strips 1 cm wide. Toss it with the peppers. Get the tortillas out of the oven. Put the beef and peppers, chopped coriander, and salsa on the table and let people fill their own tortillas.

Variations: Chicken or pork works too.

THREE CONDIMENTS
FOR CHILLI LOVERS

CHILLI OIL

Finely chop 1 hot fresh red chilli. Keep the seeds and pith if you like the extra heat. Mash it well with about 50 ml oil in a mortar with a pestle until the oil is smooth and orange-yellow. If you use a blender, more oil will be needed. For a finer, clear oil, strain it through muslin and use the bits in a stir-fry.

CHILLI VINEGAR

In Latin America and the American South, there is often a jar of vinegar and chillies on the table for fish, greens, meats, salads, and soups. Put 3–4 fresh chillies in a jar and cover with wine or cider vinegar. Top up vinegar or chillies as needed. Lasts for weeks.

DRIED CHILLI FLAKES

When chillies are plentiful, buy at least 20. Use thin-fleshed ones such as *cayenne*, not the fleshier *jalapeño*. Wash and dry them. With a needle and thread, string them together through the stem and hang them in a dry, warmish place for at least 2 weeks. When they are dry and crispy, snap off the caps. In a food-processor, or in a rough mortar and pestle, grind the chillies until the flakes are the size you want. They keep for months in a jar, but all spices lose potency with age.

PIZZA WITH ROASTED RED PEPPERS & ROSEMARY OIL

Topping pizza is so easy, so please-yourself, that it is worth mastering the crust – also simple. Try grilled or roasted courgettes, aubergines, mushrooms, fennel, leeks; wilted spinach and chard are nice too. Add pancetta, toasted pine kernels, basil strips, or chilli flakes.

SERVES 6–8

1 tbsp rosemary, finely chopped

1 tbsp olive oil

1 30-cm Pizza Crust (see p. 218)

10–12 basil leaves

4–5 tbsp Passata (see p. 215)

200 g mozzarella (a good packaged brand
  is fine; the fresh kind packed in water
  is not necessary)

4 roasted red peppers

- Cover the rosemary with the olive oil. You can do this 1–2 days ahead.
- Set the oven to 230°C.
- Make the pizza crust and flatten it in the pizza pan or on the stone.
- Chop the basil and add it to the passata. Put it into a saucepan and reduce by about half. Add a little salt.
- Shred the mozzarella with your fingers.
- Spread the passata thinly over the dough, sprinkle over the cheese, and finally lay pepper slices radiating out from the centre.
- Brush the peppers with the rosemary oil and rosemary bits.
- You can leave the pizza to rest for 30–45 minutes in a coolish place. It will rise again, and the crust will be thick and chewy. Salt lightly and bake for 20 minutes, until the dough is crispy.

PLUMS

The large rose family gives us many aromatic fruits. The flowers of cherries, plums, apricots, peaches, nectarines, pears, and apples resemble the wild rose. Remembering the seasons of tree fruits is easy. The smallest stone fruits, the cherry and apricot, come first. Middle-sized plums and peaches are in the middle, and the largest, pears and apples, are last. Britain's plum season is relatively generous, starting in July as strawberries are going, and lasting well into October, peak apple season.

Plum flesh can be red, yellow, green, pink, or a mixture. Size has much to do with whether the farmer did any thinning, a time-consuming task. When plum boughs are overloaded, small fruit result. The chief commercial varieties for eating are Japanese plums such as *Santa Rosa*. They are juicy, round, and large. The common European plum, *Agen*, is medium-sized, oval, and dark blue or red. Most are canned or dried as prunes.

Victoria is the classic British all-rounder, with yellow flesh and good acidity for cooking. When very ripe it is not bad for eating raw. *Greengage* is the British name for the French *Reine Claude*. Smallish and green with red dots, it is famous for aroma and sweetness. *Greengage* is perfect for the farmers' market: it's not a heavy cropper, it is very soft when ripe, and doesn't travel well. It cooks beautifully, too. Use a bit less sugar. *Marjorie Seedling* is a large, deep purple fruit with a blue bloom. It is good for eating raw and cooking and crops late, in October. *President* is another late-harvest cooker, large and purple.

The little, dark blue *Damson* is tart and makes famous, intense jam. The Romans dried it. A few are grown commercially, but many farmers gather them wild from dense windbreaks. The tiny yellow *Mirabelle* is also a damson type. Sloes are little black wild plums. Farmers sometimes bring them to market for sloe gin.

As with pears, many local varieties have been forgotten. Perhaps you can persuade the fruit farmer at market to grow them.

SEASON

Late July to October.

WHAT TO LOOK FOR

Smooth, unbroken skin. When ripe, soft and aromatic with almost clear skin. Wrinkling at the stem end is fine. The more bloom – silvery blush – the less it has been handled.

STORAGE

Ripen in a closed paper bag at room temperature. Ripe plums should be eaten immediately; they deteriorate quickly. If you like ripe plums ice-cold, refrigerate up to 2 days. I think it ruins the flavour and aroma.

MAKING THE MOST OF A SURPLUS

Jam and crumble.

POACHED PLUM CUSTARD TART

The recipe is for a tart, but you can eat the plums without the pastry, served with a spoonful of custard. The peppercorns are optional, but they add a spicy touch that I love.

SERVES 6–8

1 quantity Basic Pastry Cream (see p. 219)
(can be made a day ahead)
½ quantity Shortcrust Pastry with sugar,
baked blind (see p. 218)
10–12 small sweet ripe plums such as
Victoria or *Greengage*
1 vanilla pod

10–15 lavender leaves
500 ml fruity red wine
100 g Vanilla Sugar (see p. 19)
cinnamon stick
6 whole cloves
6 whole black peppercorns (optional)

- Make the pastry cream and let it cool. Make the pastry and bake it blind. Let it cool.
- Halve and stone the plums. Split the vanilla pod longways and scrape the seeds into a saucepan with the lavender leaves, wine, sugar, cinnamon, cloves, and peppercorns. If necessary, add water to cover the plums.
- Bring to the boil, then simmer until the plums are cooked but still hold their shape, about 20 minutes.
- Drain the plums well. Blot with a towel if necessary.
- Reduce the liquid to syrup, either to pour it over the fruit or to a glaze consistency for brushing the fruit in the tart, about half as much.
- Spread the custard in the cooled pastry. Lay the plum halves snugly together, cut side up to catch a bit of glaze. Brush with the glaze.

Variation: Top the custard with whole raspberries or halved strawberries, cut-side down.

> Poaching fruit in syrup is practical as well as tasty. Fruit goes mushy when cooked; sugar helps to strengthen the collapsing cell walls.

GREENGAGE SOUFFLÉ

*This is adapted from Sybil Kapoor's recipe in her wonderful book, **Simply British**.*

SERVES 4

600 g ripe greengages
4 tbsp sugar + a little extra
1 vanilla pod
1 tbsp arrowroot
large knob butter
icing sugar
5 egg whites

- Halve and stone the plums and put them with 3 tablespoons of the sugar in a saucepan. Split the vanilla pod, scrape out its seeds, and add pod and seeds to the saucepan. Cook gently until the plums are soft, 5–6 minutes, then add the arrowroot and stir until it thickens. Leave it to cool. Remove the vanilla pod, purée the plums, and sweeten further if desired. You can make this 1–2 days ahead.
- Set the oven to 220°C and put the purée into a mixing bowl.
- Melt the butter in a 1-litre soufflé dish in the oven for 1 minute. Coat the dish evenly with the butter and dust it with icing sugar. Set it aside.
- Beat the egg whites until fluffy. Add the remaining tablespoon of sugar and beat until stiff. Fold the egg whites into the purée with quick, even strokes.
- Fill the soufflé dish and smooth off the top, then sprinkle with sugar. Bake for 15 minutes or less. It will be light brown on top, 5 cm above the rim, and soft in the centre.

POTATOES

Potatoes are native to Central and South America, but it was the Irish who brought them back across the Atlantic to North America, in 1719, where they quickly replaced parsnips as the chief starch. The first big potato farms were in Londonderry, New Hampshire. Apart from the Irish, Europeans did not eat the New World potato enthusiastically for almost two hundred years.

The potato is a diverse and versatile vegetable. It suits any cooking method and any flavour. Its only limitation is that it is indigestible raw. Farmers, like cooks, get tired of the same varieties and crave novelty. Thus at farmers' markets you will find potatoes in all colours, shapes, and sizes.

Experts make finer distinctions, but the basic potato types are firm and waxy, for boiling and salads, and floury and creamy, for baking and mash. When the less starchy waxy types are cooked, the cells stay together; in floury types, they separate. To test which kind you have, make a brine solution of 11 parts water to 1 part salt. A waxy potato floats and a floury one sinks.

The potato season follows a general pattern: first new potatoes and boilers, then bakers and all-rounders, then main-crop, floury types, and finally waxy salad potatoes.

New potatoes are small tubers dug early, but some varieties, like the 1942 *Home Guard*, are best young. They have thin, slightly peeling skin and a delicate flavour. Do not peel them. Boil them and eat them with Mint Pesto (see p. 144).

A few varieties with superior flavour: *Swift* and *Maris Peer* are early boilers. *Arran Victory* is a floury type, purple with white flesh. *Cosmo* is a dense white baker. *Charlotte* and *Pink Fir Apple* (skinny, knobbly, yellow flesh) are salad potatoes; *Bintje, Aura,* and *Belle de Fontenay* are yellow-fleshed salad types; *Desirée* is an early main crop all-rounder with yellow flesh; other all-rounders are *Croft, King Edward*, the buttery *Yukon Gold,* and *Wilja*.

When possible, boil potatoes in their skins to keep nutrients and fibre. You lose less flesh by peeling after cooking. Sprouts and green patches are a build-up of alkaloids caused by exposure to light. They leave a bitter taste, so peel away green skin and flesh.

SEASON

New potatoes: May to June. Mature potatoes: through Christmas, from storage all winter.

WHAT TO LOOK FOR

Firm and heavy, with unbroken skin (except new potatoes, which are peeling). No green patches or sprouting eyes.

STORAGE

Unwashed, in a paper bag in a cool, dark place, 5–10°C. Below 5°C, the starch turns to sugar, which causes an unpleasant sweet flavour. Store apart from onions. Mature potatoes keep for months, but let the farmer do the storing. Eat new potatoes within a week.

MAKING THE MOST OF A SURPLUS

Mash and soup are good fresh, but have an unpleasant texture when frozen.

PINK FIR APPLES WITH PERFECT SHALLOT VINAIGRETTE

Pink Fir Apples are long, skinny, knobbly, and waxy. A late cropper – you find them at market in the dead of winter. Make the dressing at least 2 hours before, or better still, overnight. It keeps well for 4–5 days, getting mellower.

100 g *Pink Fir Apples* or other waxy
  salad potato, such as *Bintje*,
  Purple Congo or *Charlotte*, per person,
  scrubbed and cut into bite-sized pieces
1 quantity of Perfect Shallot Vinaigrette
  (see p. 189)

- Boil the potatoes in salted water until just cooked, but intact.
- Put all the dressing ingredients into a small jar and shake vigorously.
- Toss the potatoes with the dressing, season to taste and serve warm.

CRAB SALAD WITH NEW POTATOES

*Small new potatoes such as **Home Guard** work here. So would **Pink Fir Apple** or **Delikatesse**.*

SERVES 2

1 tbsp parsley, finely chopped

½ spring onion, white and green part
  finely chopped

3 tbsp best olive oil

2 tsp lemon juice

¼ tsp paprika

scant ¼ tsp ground cayenne (optional)

100 g new potatoes, scrubbed, halved
  and cooked in salted water

200 g fresh crab meat

100 g corn kernels, cooked

2 large handfuls lettuce or watercress

- Mix together the parsley and spring onion with 2 tablespoons of the olive oil, the lemon juice, and spices, and season to taste.
- Mix the crab with the corn, potatoes, and the dressing. Season.
- Toss the leaves with the remaining tablespoon of olive oil and top with the crab.

SPANISH TORTILLA

The Spanish baked omelette is delicious hot or cold.

SERVES 2–4

2 medium *Russet* potatoes, peeled
  and diced
1 yellow onion, diced
4 large cloves garlic, finely chopped
1 tbsp olive oil
6 eggs

- Boil the diced potatoes in salted water until almost cooked, 6–8 minutes, and drain.
- In an ovenproof frying-pan, sauté the onion and the garlic in the olive oil until they are soft. Add the potatoes and mix well.
- Beat the eggs and season them. Pour them over the vegetables, tilting the pan to coat. Cover, and cook over a low heat until set, about 12 minutes depending on how deep the pan is.
- Heat the grill. Put the pan under the grill until the top of the tortilla is light brown, 2–3 minutes. Cool partially before eating. Delicious drizzled with Basil Oil (see p. 112).

Variations: Add 100 g chopped, steamed spinach to the egg mixture. Or sauté 75 g chopped mushrooms with the onion. Or sauté 1 large red or yellow pepper, diced, with the onion.

OCTOPUS WITH
POTATOES & PAPRIKA

Tender octopus with potatoes and paprika is a common tapa in Spain. It is hard to find the ones with large tentacles in Britain, but little ones from Devon are delicious. If you cannot find fresh octopus, use tinned ones packed in oil and drain well; 250 g canned makes a salad for 2. You will find smoked paprika in a Spanish delicatessen, if not in the supermarket.

SERVES 6–8

4 kg octopus, untrimmed

500 g waxy salad potatoes, such as
   Pink Fir Apple, Delikatesse or
   Belle de Fontenay

2 tbsp smoked paprika

3–4 tbsp best olive oil

• Ask the fishmonger to clean the octopus. At home, rinse it well in several changes of cold water. Boil a large saucepan of water and cook the octopus until it is tender, at least 1 hour. It's ready when you can easily press a knife into the skirt, the thickest bit where the head meets the legs. It can be prepared a day ahead. (Save the water for fish stock.)

• Cut the big, balloon-like head from the cluster of legs with suckers. Slice the legs into rounds. (Freeze head for stock if you like.)

• Slice the potatoes into small rounds and boil in salted water until just tender but intact. Drain and toss them with the octopus, paprika, and olive oil. Season and serve at room temperature. It is delicious the next day.

Variation: If you vary the quantity, use half cooked potatoes and half cooked octopus by volume. Adding 2 handfuls of Oven-dried Tomatoes, oil drained (see p. 213) makes a wonderful salad. Or use Garlic-in-Oil (see p. 219).

PUMPKINS & WINTER SQUASHES

Unlike summer squashes, pumpkins and winter squashes are allowed to reach full maturity, with viable seeds and hard rinds for retaining moisture in storage. The flesh is dense and sweet compared with the tender, insubstantial flesh of immature courgettes and summer squashes.

Pumpkins are pretty, but winter squashes like butternut taste better. Pumpkins have a larger seed cavity and relatively less flesh than winter squashes and their flesh is blander and less dense. Large pumpkins are spongy and meant only for jack o' lanterns. Only the smaller pumpkins, such as *Small Sugar* and *Jack be Little*, are good to eat, but even they are not what is in the tinned pumpkin Americans use for Thanksgiving pies. That is the denser and sweeter flesh of the neck pumpkin, a kind of butternut. Nevertheless a pie pumpkin has a delicate, distinct flavour, unlike the other winter squashes, and it is nice roasted.

Winter squashes can be divided unscientifically into three camps. One sort has a round, bark-like stem like *Buttercup*, the other a thinner, sharper fluted stem, like a pumpkin. In general, the buttercup types have drier, smoother, sweeter flesh. They include the scrumptious onion squash or Japanese pumpkin (*Red Kuri*), large hubbards (*Blue Ballet* and *Golden Hubbard*), and *Sweet Mama*, another buttercup type.

Fluted-stem squashes include the heart-shaped, green or golden *Acorn* and *Delicata*, an oblong, green and white striped variety. Both have less flavour and pale, sometimes stringy, flesh. The butternut is a third type. It has a fluted stem too, but the orange flesh is sweet, rich, and dense. *Cobnut* was bred for the British climate.

Pink Jumbo Banana is a wonderful pink squash with tasty, creamy flesh. *Vegetable spaghetti* has a yellow rind. When boiled, it breaks up into pale yellow filaments – novel texture, but bland.

Pumpkins are best roasted or in soup. Winter squash is delicious roasted, baked, grilled, or puréed. The meaty winter squashes can be substituted for each other in almost any recipe, but the flavour, and to some degree texture, will differ. Like all bright vegetables, winter squash is packed with vitamin A, second only to carrots.

SEASON
Pumpkins: September to November. Winter squashes: late August, then from storage until February or March.

WHAT TO LOOK FOR
Firm, heavy squashes with unbroken skin. Butternut should be an even pinkish tan without a background tinge of green. Stems dry and firmly attached.

STORAGE
Pumpkins keep a month or so at 10–15°C, winter squashes for several months. Never refrigerate.

MAKING THE MOST OF A SURPLUS
They store well, so it scarcely matters, but purée is convenient and freezes well.

PINK JUMBO BANANA
& WHITE BEAN SOUP

This mild, delicious winter squash looks like a giant, creamy pink banana. The recipe works with any flavourful winter squash, such as butternut or onion squash, but the taste will be different. The soup is half-puréed, so it is creamy-chunky. Custom-made stock intensifies the flavour.

SERVES 4–6

4 kg *Pink Jumbo Banana*, with seeds

3 tbsp olive oil + a little extra

200 g dried *shiitake, porcini* or *cèpes*,
   or 400 g fresh mushrooms

2 shallots, finely chopped

2 x 400 g tins cannellini beans

³/₄ tsp salt

pepper

soft goat's cheese and toast (optional)

For the stock

1 yellow onion

2 large sprigs each rosemary and sage

3 cloves garlic

1 bay leaf

- First make the stock. Quarter but do not peel the onion. Smash but do not peel the garlic. Reserve 1 tablespoon of each of the rosemary and sage, finely chopped. Chop the remaining herbs roughly, with their stems. Heat the garlic, onion, bay, herbs, and squash seeds with the flesh in the olive oil, poking with a wooden spoon until they are soft and aromatic, about 20 minutes.
- Add 1 litre water and simmer, uncovered, until the stock is flavourful, at least 25 minutes. It can be made 1 day ahead, but don't strain it until you want to use it.
- While the stock simmers, set the oven to 220°C. Cut the squash into large chunks, and coat the cut sides with olive oil. Bake it cut-side down on a baking sheet until it is soft, at least 1 hour. You can do this one day ahead. Peel it, purée two-thirds, and dice the rest.
- Soak the dried mushrooms in 300 ml water for at least 20 minutes. Drain, and squeeze out the moisture.
- Sauté the mushrooms, shallots, and reserved chopped herbs with the olive oil in a large saucepan. When they are soft add the cannellini beans and their juice. Season, and simmer until the liquid is thick and creamy, mashing a few beans. Remove the pan from the heat.
- In a large pot, heat the beans and the squash, the whole bean mixture, the mushrooms and most of the stock. Add the diced squash last so that it stays intact. Thin with more stock, and season.
- If you like, add a spoonful of cream or olive oil, and serve with toast spread with soft goat's cheese.

BUTTERNUT RISOTTO

SERVES 4–6

2.5 kg butternut squash

2 yellow onions

4 large cloves garlic

4 tbsp olive oil

1 bay leaf

4–5 sprigs dried summer savoury or thyme, or 1 heaped tbsp, crumbled

1/2 tsp salt

300 g Arborio or other short-grain rice

good Parmesan for grating

- Set the oven to 180°C.
- Quarter the squashes and scoop out their seeds. Brush the flesh with olive oil, salt it lightly and roast until soft, about 45 minutes. Scoop out the flesh and purée it.
- Make the stock with the peels and any trimmings. Quarter but do not peel 1 of the onions and smash but do not peel 2 of the cloves of garlic. Put them with 2 tablespoons of the oil, the bay leaf, herbs, the squash pulp and seeds in a large pan. When they begin to smell aromatic, add 2 litres of water and half of the salt. Boil, then simmer until it has reduced to about 1.5 litres, about 30 minutes. Strain.
- While the squash and the stock cook, finely chop the remaining onion and the garlic.
- When you are ready to cook the rice, have the stock simmering, and sauté the garlic and onions in the remaining olive oil until they are soft.
- Add the puréed squash and stir well. Put in the rice and stir to coat.
- Reduce the heat and add the hot stock in small amounts as it's absorbed, constantly scraping the bottom, 20–25 minutes. When the rice is tender but not mushy and the sauce is creamy, you can stir in grated cheese, a bit of butter, olive oil, or cream. Season to taste.

BAKED ONION SQUASH WITH HAZELNUTS

SERVES 4

1 medium onion squash

about 24 hazelnuts, crushed

4 scant tsp butter

4 scant tsp Demerara sugar

- Set the oven to 180°C. Quarter the squash and scoop out the seeds; save them for stock. Bake the squash until it is soft, about 30 minutes depending on thickness.
- When the squash is almost done, warm the nuts, butter, and sugar in a saucepan. When the butter has melted, spread the mixture evenly over the squash and bake for another 10 minutes.

BUTTERNUT PURÉE

This easy recipe is served as a thick mound of mash or diluted for soup.

SERVES 4–6

3 kg butternut squash

2 tbsp olive oil

2 cloves garlic, smashed but not peeled

1 bay leaf

1 large sprig rosemary, roughly chopped

500 ml–1 litre water

½ tsp salt

freshly grated nutmeg

24 sage leaves, whole

- Set the oven to 180°C. Split the butternut lengthways and scoop out the seeds and pulp. Cut in large chunks, oil lightly, and bake until soft, which takes about 1 hour. Or cut the squash in half, pierce it a few times with a fork, and bake it cut side down.
- Heat 1 tablespoon of the oil in a large saucepan. Add the garlic, a few chunks of the squash, the bay leaf, rosemary, and squash seeds. When it begins to smell aromatic, add the water and salt and simmer uncovered for about 25 minutes, until reduced by about half for a purée, but less for soup.
- Scoop the butternut out of its skin and, while it is still warm, any syrup out of the pan. Purée it with the stock and the remaining olive oil. Add nutmeg and season to taste.
- Top purée with whole fried sage leaves or bread dipped in rosemary oil: chop the rosemary finely and cover it with olive oil. It lasts for 2 weeks in a cool pantry. Strain the pungent green oil and put it on a saucer with good bread.

ROASTED ONION SQUASH WITH SAGE

SERVES 2–4

1 kg onion squash (800 g trimmed)

2 tbsp sage, finely chopped, no stems

4 tbsp olive oil

- Set the oven to 240°C. Chop the squash into quarters, peel it, and scoop out the seeds (save them for stock). Chop into quarters again and slice it into crescent shapes, about 1 x 2 cm thick.
- Mix the squash, sage, and oil in a shallow baking tin with your hands. Salt it well (squash is all starch), mix again, and bake for 10 minutes at 240°C, until it browns. Then reduce the heat to 200°C and cook for another 10 minutes or until soft.

RASPBERRIES &
BLACKBERRIES

I asked my brother Charles what he remembered about eating on the farm. Immediately he mentioned one of my most vivid associations: red raspberries and Sunday mornings. On Sunday mornings at 6 o'clock we picked raspberries for the Takoma Park market. For selling delicate produce, nothing beats a sign saying PICKED TODAY. When the market truck left, we picked one more punnet for raspberry pancakes with raspberry syrup. The syrup was simply berries boiled with sugar until they fell apart.

The bramble berries are compound fruits made up of many tiny fruits called drupelets. Like all delicate, perishable foods, they are best with very little done to them. Don't even wash them. Once ripe they spoil rapidly and must be eaten – no messing about. If you're lucky enough to have a lot, make jam, summer pudding or a pie.

Size should not affect flavour, but over-irrigating can produce large, bland berries. Red, yellow, orange, and even cream-coloured raspberries have a similar flavour. *Allgold* (yellow) and *Autumn Bliss* (red) taste good. Raspberries grown in poly-tunnels appear as early as May, but the better-tasting ones are the main outdoor crop in late June. The less common black raspberry is smaller and less juicy, with a more intense flavour.

Blackberries are sturdier and tart, with a distinct, sometimes stronger flavour. Unlike the raspberry, which is hollow in the middle, the blackberry is solid, and can be a bit crunchy. *Ashton Cross* and *Fantasia* are good varieties. Inconveniently, blackberries turn black before they are fully ripe, so it is hard to tell if they are ready, and underripe berries are positively sour. Ripe ones are midnight black and very soft.

Most of the thousand known blackberry varieties are wild. They grow all over Britain and farmers sometimes bring them to market. They are smaller and less juicy than cultivated ones, but have a better flavour. They make a delicious crumble with almonds, hazelnuts, or Kent cobnuts.

Loganberries and boysenberries are blackberry-raspberry hybrids named after their creators.

SEASON

Blackberries: mid-July to September. Wild blackberries: August to October.
Raspberries: early June to October, peaking July to September.

WHAT TO LOOK FOR

Whole berries, no broken seeds bleeding red juice, no mould. Tiny hairs are visible when they've been handled very little. Blackberries and black raspberries must be deep black, no violet. Red raspberries must be dark pink all over.

STORAGE

Don't wash. Discard mouldy berries and put in one layer on kitchen paper. Eat immediately at room temperature. Refrigerate overnight if necessary.

MAKING THE MOST OF A SURPLUS

Syrup (see p. 175) and Jam (see p. 197). Freeze whole berries on a flat tin, then bag them. Macerated berries: sprinkle with sugar and keep cool.

RASPBERRY MERINGUES

When you are making Custard (see p. 218) or Mayonnaise (see p. 218), use the egg whites for meringues.

MAKES about 40 meringues

6 large or 8 smaller egg, whites only

50 ml strained Raspberry Syrup (see below)

2 tbsp sugar

$^1/_2$ tsp vanilla extract

- Set oven to 125 °C. Generously oil or butter two large baking sheets to stop the meringues sticking.
- Beat the egg whites until fluffy. Add the sugar and beat until they form stiff peaks.
- Add the vanilla to the syrup. Swiftly fold the syrup into the egg whites. Drop even spoonfuls of the mixture on the trays. The meringues will not spread or rise, so try to achieve relatively quickly the shape you want.
- Bake for 1$^1/_2$ hours. They should be light brown on the bottom and stiff to the touch.
- Allow the meringues to cool completely in the oven. Do not stack them until they are completely dry.

Variations: Try strawberry or blackberry syrup.

RASPBERRY SYRUP

Raspberry syrup freezes well. With seeds, it is delicious in smoothies, yoghurt, all-raspberry summer pudding or on toast and pancakes. I like a tart syrup, but you can add more sugar if you like. Cooking time is a minimum of 20 minutes, but if you want it thicker, you can reduce it. You can also make syrup with blackberries or blueberries.

MAKES about 1.5–2 litres

1 vanilla pod (optional)

1.5 kg red or black raspberries

200 g sugar

- Split the vanilla pod if using, scrape out the seeds, and put them with the pod in a large saucepan. Heat the raspberries and sugar gently until they are cooked, at least 20 minutes. Add more sugar to taste.
- Strain the seeds for clear raspberry syrup and use leftover pulp in berry crumble.
- It will keep in the fridge for a week. Or freeze it in 100-ml quantities.

RASPBERRY BUTTERMILK PANCAKES WITH RASPBERRY SYRUP

When there is time to cook breakfast at the farm, we make fruit pancakes. Buttermilk is skimmed cultured milk. Its acidity helps the pancakes rise. Half yoghurt, half milk is a good substitute.

For perfect pancakes, do not over-beat the batter; after mixing, refrigerate it for 3–6 hours; when you cook them use a hot griddle or heavy frying-pan and make sure that the heat is evenly distributed.

MAKES 8 x 10-cm pancakes

150 g flour
1 tsp baking powder
¼ tsp salt
250 ml buttermilk
1 egg
2 tbsp oil
about 200 g raspberries

- In a good-sized bowl, stir the dry ingredients together well. In another bowl, whisk the wet ingredients, then pour the mixture into the flour. Mix well, but as little as possible. Cover and refrigerate for 3–6 hours.
- Oil and heat a griddle or frying-pan. Use a 50-pence-piece-sized drop of oil per batch of 4. A few drops of cold water should sizzle and sputter when it's hot enough. If it sits there, it's too cold; if it vanishes, it's too hot.
- Mix the fruit with the batter. Allow the batter to drip from the tip of a spoon in 4 even circles.
- The pancakes are ready to flip in 3–4 minutes. When bubbles appear on the surface, see if the pancake is browned and flip it. The second side takes half as long to cook and does not brown evenly. Eat immediately with butter and Raspberry Syrup (see p. 175).

Variation: Substitute blueberries, blackberries, strawberries or 2 medium apples or pears (diced not peeled) for the raspberries; add 2 tablespoons broken walnuts, almonds or pecans; try ½ tsp vanilla or almond extract.

WILD BLACKBERRY
& APPLE CRUMBLE

Wild blackberries are smaller and more intense-tasting than cultivated ones. This crumble freezes well.

SERVES 2–4

200 g wild blackberries

1 large *Bramley*, diced

3 tbsp apple juice

1 tsp pure almond extract

2 tbsp + 1 tsp Demerara sugar

1 tbsp plain flour

2 tbsp porridge oats

2 tbsp flaked or finely crushed almonds

2 large knobs soft butter

freshly grated nutmeg

- Mix together the fruit, apple juice, almond extract, and one teaspoon of sugar. Spread it in a small baking tin.
- Set the oven to 180°C.
- With your fingers, rub the butter into the dry ingredients. Spread the topping over the fruit and bake for about 20 minutes, until the berries bubble and the top is crispy and golden.

BLACKBERRY PIE

SERVES 6–8

700 g blackberries

175 g sugar

3 tbsp cornflour

$\frac{1}{2}$ tsp almond extract

1 quantity Shortcrust Pastry (which makes
  top and bottom crusts) (see p. 218)

vanilla ice cream, to serve

- Mix the berries with the sugar, cornflour, and almond extract until a glaze forms. Let it stand for 15 minutes.
- Line a 22-cm baking tin with half of the pastry. Fill it with the berries. Lay the pastry lid over the top, and pinch the edges with your thumb and forefinger to close them. Make at least 4 crosses in the crust to allow the steam to escape.
- Bake at 180°C for 20 minutes. Move the pie to the other oven rack, so it browns evenly, and bake for 25 minutes more. Sprinkle with sugar and cool before serving with ice cream.

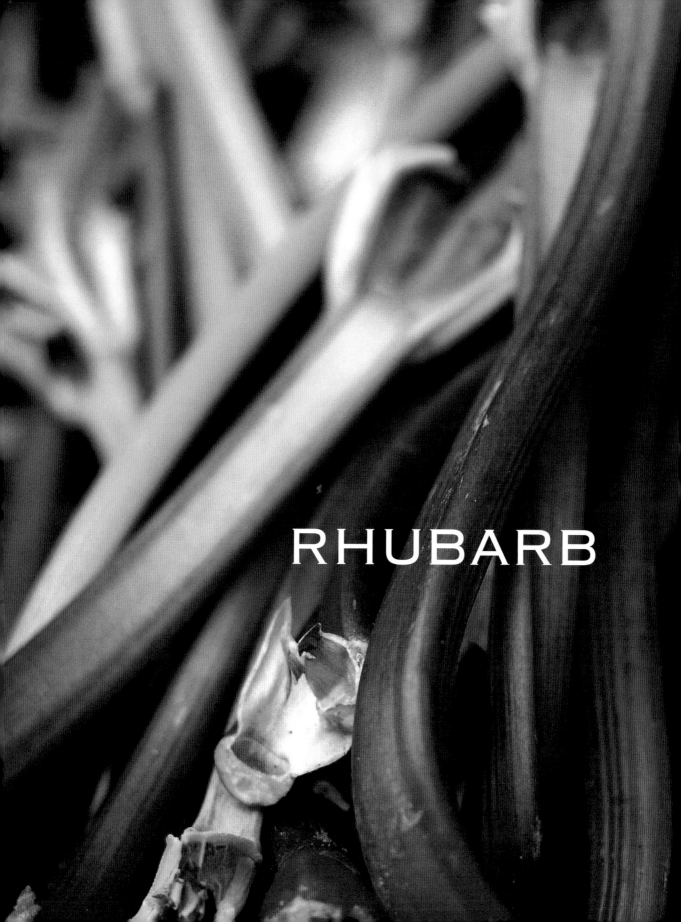

RHUBARB

Rhubarb is an Asian vegetable, unexpectedly in the buckwheat family. It is difficult to imagine who first cooked the tart, fruity pink and green stalks. European cooks didn't use rhubarb until the eighteenth century, and it was another hundred years before Americans did. Rhubarb stalks are high in potassium and vitamin C, but the enormous leaves, seldom seen at market, are toxic.

To understand this unusual vegetable, it helps to know how rhubarb grows. Its cultivation is somewhat analogous to that of asparagus (see p. 33). It is a perennial that sends up shoots or stalks from a root called a crown. When rhubarb stalks are about 30 cms tall, the farmer pulls them and cuts off the leaf. A large crown produces a thick stalk, a smaller crown a thin one. Thick or thin, all stalks are tender when cooked.

In mid-summer, when the crowns are depleted, all the stalks are thin and rhubarb season ends. Why? The farmer could cut rhubarb stalks all summer, but only at the price of reducing next year's crop. Rhubarb leaves manufacture food by photosynthesis to feed the crown. Picking the stalks indefinitely would prevent the regeneration of the crown.

Pink, red or green, all the stalks are fruity. Some varieties are redder, others mostly green. You may see pale pink rhubarb in the shops before it turns up at the market. It has been forced – warmed to bring it on early – and is pale because it has been kept in the dark. Local farmers have ways of extending the rhubarb season, too. An early crop can be grown under poly-tunnels, and the later crop kept cool under a deep mulch until the farmer wants to start picking, when it is uncovered and allowed to reach full colour. Peak season rhubarb grown in the open field has the most flavour. Think of its classic partner – strawberries – and cook them together when their peak overlaps in June.

How tart do you like it? This is the only question with rhubarb, and it is really only important with pies, because you can't taste the pie before it is cooked. With stewed rhubarb, soufflé, or sorbet, you can add sugar to taste.

A chunk of raw rhubarb is wonderful in fruit juices, especially apple. Peel off the outer strings, so they don't tie up the blender or juicer. The pale green centre is still fruity.

SEASON

February to July. The open field crop in peak season, March to May, has the most flavour.

WHAT TO LOOK FOR

Stiff, not rubbery stalks. Freshly cut ends, not white from healing over.

STORAGE

In a plastic bag in the fridge for about a week.

MAKING THE MOST OF A SURPLUS

Stewed rhubarb keeps for about 10 days in the fridge and freezes well. Delicious with vanilla yoghurt or ice cream. Fresh rhubarb can be frozen for pies and purées. Wash, dry, cut into chunks and freeze in bags.

RHUBARB SOUFFLÉ

In modern ovens, the temperamental soufflé is easy. Use a 1-litre soufflé dish.

SERVES 4

600 g rhubarb, washed and trimmed of its
   leaves, cut in 3-cm pieces
100 g + 1 tbsp Vanilla Sugar (see p.19),
   and a little extra
1 vanilla pod
1 tbsp arrowroot
large knob unsalted butter
icing sugar
5 egg whites

- Put the rhubarb in a saucepan with the 100 g vanilla sugar.
- Split the vanilla pod with a small knife and scrape the seeds into the pan. Add the pod and heat gently until rhubarb has collapsed, about 15 minutes. After about 5 minutes, add the arrowroot and mix well.
- Cool the rhubarb and remove the vanilla pod. (At this stage, the mixture can be refrigerated for 2 days or frozen.)
- Set the oven to 220°C.
- Heat the butter in the soufflé dish in the oven. As soon as it has melted, spread it all over the sides of the dish and dust with icing sugar.
- Beat the egg whites until they are fluffy. Add the remaining tablespoon of vanilla sugar and beat until stiff.
- With a rubber spatula, quickly and gently fold the rhubarb into the egg whites, mixing well.
- Fill the soufflé dish, then smooth off the top and sprinkle with sugar.
- Bake for about 15 minutes without peeking into the oven. It should be brown on top, 4–5 cm above the rim, and soft in the centre. Eat before it sinks.

STEWED RHUBARB WITH GINGER

SERVES 4

600 g rhubarb, trimmed and cut in
  4-cm pieces

100 g sugar

1 vanilla pod

1-cm chunk ginger, peeled in ribbons with
  a vegetable peeler

- Heat all the ingredients gently until the rhubarb collapses, about 15 minutes. Do not be tempted to add water, otherwise you will need to strain it (see below). It should be thick but pourable, not runny.
- This keeps in the fridge for about a week and freezes well.

Spin-off: Rhubarb syrup makes a lovely drink. This stewed rhubarb recipe, strained, makes about 200 ml rhubarb syrup. Mix 100 ml with a glass of sparkling wine or lemonade.

Variation: Candied rhubarb is delicious on vanilla ice cream. Boil 100 g vanilla sugar with 15 peeled ginger ribbons (use a vegetable peeler) in 2 tablespoons of water until it makes a stretchy candy floss when you pull it with a spoon. Add 400 g of chopped rhubarb and cook until it is soft. Do not break up the pieces.

RHUBARB PIE

How tart you like it is a matter of taste. With less sugar, you get more fruity rhubarb flavour. Use 300 g sugar if you have a sweet tooth.

SERVES 6–8

800 g rhubarb, washed, trimmed and
  cut into 4-cm lengths

1 quantity Shortcrust Pastry (for top and
  bottom crusts) (see p. 218)

250 g sugar

1/2 tsp vanilla

2 tbsp water

3 tbsp cornflour

vanilla ice cream

- Set the oven to 180°C.
- Line a baking tin with half of the pastry.
- Mix all the other ingredients until a glaze forms, and pour into the tin. Lay the pastry lid over the top, pinching the edges closed between your thumb and forefinger. Make at least 4 crosses in the pastry with a knife so that steam can escape when the rhubarb collapses.
- Bake for 20 minutes, then move the pie to the other rack in the oven so that it browns evenly and bake for 25 minutes more.
- When cool, serve with vanilla ice cream.

SALAD LEAVES

'A salad is not a meal,' said American writer Fran Lebowitz. 'It is a style.' Even good restaurants get green salads wrong. If you like salads, you will make good ones. Every bite, whether leaf or vegetable, must be well washed and dried, bite-sized, and evenly coated with dressing. Herbs must be finely chopped.

Do not limit yourself to baby leaves. As with most vegetables, if the leaves grew fast, unchecked by heat or drought, they will be tender, even when they are large. The darker the leaf (red or green), the more vitamins it contains.

There are four kinds of lettuce: head or cabbage, loose-leaf, crisp, and *Cos*. Farmers sell loose-leaf varieties in heads or as loose leaves. Excellent varieties are *Lollo Rossa, Salad Bowl*, and the oak-leaf *Red Cocarde*. Head lettuces are more tightly packed, with a pale heart at the centre. Try *Buttercrunch*, red *Burgundy Boston*, or the ever-popular Victorian *Tom Thumb*. *Iceberg* is not the supermarket variety but the original crisp type, with red-tinged leaves and excellent flavour. *Little Gem* is the best-tasting Cos.

Lettuces are only half of the salad, though, and farmers bring many other greens to market. Many are peppery. Wild rocket is feathery and hotter than common salad rocket, which has rounder, thicker leaves. *American* or *Land* cress is like watercress, with flat, dark green, peppery leaves. *Greek* and *Fine Curled* cress are similar but curly. Mâche or lamb's lettuce (*Verte de Cambrai*) makes a small rosette of mild leaves.

Summer purslane (*Golden* or *Green*) is wild or cultivated. Its fleshy pink and green stems and leaves are citrussy in salads. Or steam it like beet greens, with olive oil and vinegar. *Claytonia*, or winter purslane, contains much more vitamin C than lettuce and can also be cooked like spinach. Radicchio is a slightly bitter, bright scarlet and white leaf, with a loose or tight head. Use it and endive sparingly. Edible flowers include violas, marigolds, and nasturtium petals with their succulent, peppery leaves. Wild ramson, often called wild garlic, has a tall green leaf and white flowers, which both give salads and sautés a garlicky flavour.

See Asian Greens (p. 26) for other crunchy and peppery salad leaves.

SEASON

All year, including leaves grown under poly-tunnels and row covers. Head lettuce up to Christmas. By mid-March and early April, oak leaf and rocket. By mid-May, round lettuce again. Winter purslane, cress, and mâche all winter.

WHAT TO LOOK FOR

Perky leaves. No bruises or creases. Whole plant if possible.

STORAGE

Don't wash until you eat. Keep in fridge in a plastic bag with a bit of air in it. Use in 1–3 days. A whole lettuce head and sturdier greens such as purslane keep longer.

MAKING THE MOST OF A SURPLUS

Large salads, lots of them. They don't keep or freeze well.

HOW TO MAKE A PERFECT GREEN SALAD

Nothing is worse than a wilted salad.

- Store leaves unwashed with stems or as heads until the day you eat them.
- You can wash leaves up to a day before serving. Dry whole leaves well, put them into a plastic bag and tie it tightly, leaving some air in it, and keep it in the fridge.

Nothing is worse than a gritty or watery salad.

- Fill a large vessel with cold water. Dunk the leaves, swish them round, and remove them by the handful, allowing water to drain from your hands before putting the leaves into a colander.
- Refill the bowl with clean water and repeat, several times if necessary to remove all grit.
- Do not pour the water out through the leaves or the grit will catch in them.
- Dry the leaves in a salad spinner, a few at a time. Never dress a wet salad. Oil and water do not mix.

Nothing is worse than a badly dressed salad.

- Do not tear leaves into bite-sized pieces until immediately before dressing and serving.
- Most leaves should be dressed immediately before eating. Otherwise the oil soaks through, weighing them down. Exceptions, such as watercress, are noted in the recipe.
- Every leaf, shred of crab and crumb of feta must be lightly and evenly coated with dressing.
- You need one tool – a very large salad bowl – and the old rule: toss salad 100 times. Fifty is okay. Your hands are best, or two large spoons.

ROCKET, WATERCRESS & TOMATO SALAD

There are two ways to handle stemmy salad greens: remove the stems, or, if they are tender, chop them up and eat them. This is the chopped version; watercress and rocket stems are just as peppery as the leaves.

SERVES 2–4

100 g rocket	1 tbsp + 1 tsp best olive oil
100 g watercress	2 tsp balsamic vinegar
3 medium tomatoes (about 400 g)	salt

- Chop the greens with their stems. Dice the tomatoes. Shake the dressing ingredients in a jar, pour over the salad, toss and season.

PASTA WITH WILD ROCKET & PANCETTA

I do not think much of wild rocket in salads: too much stem, too little leaf, and not much difference in flavour from the standard salad rocket. But wilted, almost like a herb, it is delicious. Mizuna, a stemmy Asian mustard, would also work.

150–200 g short pasta per person

125 g wild rocket per person, stems trimmed

65 g pancetta per person, diced

1 tbsp + 1 tsp olive oil per person

- Cook the pasta in salted water.
- When it is half done, fry the pancetta gently with a little olive oil in a large frying-pan until it has browned, 4–5 minutes.
- Add the rocket and a little more oil. Stir until it has wilted but is still bright green, about 2 minutes.
- Drain the pasta, tip it into the frying-pan, and stir. Add the remaining olive oil and season.

Variation: Add 2–3 Oven-dried Tomatoes (see p. 213) per person, chopped into bite-sized pieces and use the orange-coloured tomato oil from the jar instead of olive oil.

POACHED SALMON & WATERCRESS SALAD

Also delicious with chicken or crabmeat. For delicate crab, use lemon juice instead of sherry vinegar.

SERVES 2

2 salmon fillets

150 ml white wine

1 clove garlic, smashed and peeled

1 bay leaf

400 g watercress, leaves, picked over and chopped

1 quantity Sherry Vinaigrette (see p. 189)

- Poach the salmon in the wine with the garlic and bay leaf until it is just rose-pink at the centre. Drain. When it is cool, flake it with a fork into chunks.
- Toss the watercress with the dressing and season it. Gently mix in the salmon.

FIVE VINAIGRETTES

In all vinaigrettes, the ratio of vinegar (or fruit juice) to oil should be 1 to 3 or 4. The quantities given below coat 1 head for 2 people who love salad or more modest salads for 4. Put all the ingredients into a jar and shake well. Add salt and pepper to taste.

SHERRY VINAIGRETTE

3–4 tbsp best olive oil

1 tbsp sherry vinegar

½ shallot, finely chopped

1 tsp chopped chives and flowers (optional)

1 tsp honey

LEMON BASIL VINAIGRETTE

Good on warm asparagus too.

3–4 tbsp best olive oil

1 tbsp fresh lemon juice

1 small shallot

1 small clove garlic, smashed, peeled
 and finely chopped

10–12 lemon basil leaves, finely chopped

FENNEL VINAIGRETTE

3–4 tbsp best olive oil

1 tbsp fennel leaves or the herb, fennel,
 finely chopped

1 tbsp white wine vinegar

½ large bulb fennel, finely chopped

1 small shallot, finely chopped

HONEY LEMON DRESSING

This is good on rocket and cress too. Use plenty of black pepper.

3 tbsp avocado oil

1 tbsp fresh lemon juice

2 tsp honey, warmed if not already runny

PERFECT SHALLOT VINAIGRETTE

Leave the shallots in the oil for at least 2 hours to make them mellow.

1 shallot, finely chopped

3 tbsp best olive oil

2 tsp white wine or champagne vinegar

1 tsp Dijon mustard

SPINACH

Spinach has a smooth, velvety texture and a mild, distinctive flavour. In salads, it is more substantial than lettuce and holds up to stronger flavours like bacon, but when steamed it is as tender as any leaf, with a flavour as delicate as asparagus. In deepest winter it is a rare green vegetable and delicious raw. It flavours sauces almost like a herb and makes a lovely soup. All that, and spinach is one of the dark, leafy greens one is exhorted to eat. That is because it is rich in folic acid, iron, vitamins A, magnesium, and potassium. You can't beat spinach.

Spinach comes in smooth and wrinkly varieties. I prefer the very curly kind for that thick, succulent bite that distinguishes it from lettuce. All spinach, and especially the curly kind, must be washed thoroughly to remove grit from its crevices. Use the method described on page 186, and repeat several times if necessary. Dry it well in a salad spinner.

There are lots of edible *faux* spinaches, many of them delicious. Perpetual spinach (also called leaf beet) is a winter-hardy cousin to beetroot and chard. Cook it like Swiss chard. New Zealand spinach is another imposter, with thick, heart-shaped leaves. *Orach* (*Golden* and *Red Plume*) is a lovely climbing vine with a tasty heart-shaped leaf. *Strawberry* spinach is another vine with small red berries and spinach-like leaves. Both leaf and berry are edible, but it is mainly decorative.

Spinach is delicious with cheese, yoghurt, eggs, nutmeg, chick peas, lentils, and cannellini beans. It is best cooked briefly, including its tender stems. Cook it in just the water left on the leaves after washing or sauté until wilted. Dress with olive oil and lemon. It should be bright green. Add to beans, soups, and stews late in the cooking. A purée of steamed spinach with soft cheese makes a pretty pasta sauce. Summer purslane, a succulent wild and cultivated plant with a strong lemon flavour (see p. 185), is a good match for steamed spinach.

Buy more spinach than you think you need. One person easily eats 250 g raw, or twice that cooked. One chemical peculiarity: like most dark leafy greens, spinach contains lots of calcium, but its high levels of oxalic acid (also present in rhubarb) prevent its absorption.

SEASON

All year. Peak season: May to November.

WHAT TO LOOK FOR

Bright, dark green leaves, no yellow. Crisp not rubbery stems.

STORAGE

Don't wash or trim stems. Refrigerate in a plastic bag with some air.
Eat in 3–4 days.

MAKING THE MOST OF A SURPLUS

Soup and purée. It isn't worth canning or freezing spinach.

QUICK GARLIC & SPINACH SOUP

SERVES 2

500 g spinach, washed

4 cloves garlic, smashed, peeled, and
finely chopped

2 tbsp olive oil

1 tsp tahini

75–100 ml milk or cream

- Sauté the garlic in 1 tablespoon of the olive oil until it is soft. Add the wet spinach, cover, and cook until the leaves are wilted but still bright green.
- Purée the spinach with the remaining olive oil and the tahini. Stir in milk until you reach your preferred thickness, then adjust the seasoning.

SPINACH SALAD WITH PEARS & HAZELNUTS

SERVES 4

125 g hazelnuts, crushed lightly

500 g spinach, washed, dried,
and stems trimmed

2 tbsp + 1 tsp hazelnut oil

4 *Comice* pears, firm but ripe, cored and
cut into bite-sized pieces

- Gently toast the hazelnuts in a dry frying-pan. Do not let them burn. Remove them from the pan and set them aside.
- In a large bowl, toss the spinach with the oil until it is completely coated. Season and toss again.
- Put in the nuts and pears, toss briefly and serve.

WILTED SPINACH WITH PINE KERNELS

Cooking destroys the nutrients of cold-pressed vegetable, nut, and seed oils. As far as possible, add them at the end. Topped with a poached egg, this makes a light meal.

1–2 tbsp pine kernels per person, to taste

1 tbsp olive oil per person

150 g spinach per person, washed
and stems trimmed

- Toast the pine kernels in a dry frying-pan over a low heat, shaking the pan to brown them on all sides. Do not let them burn. Remove them from the pan.
- Add the wet spinach in the pan and cover. Stir once or twice until the leaves are wilted but bright green, 4–5 minutes.
- Toss the spinach well with olive oil and salt. Served it topped with the pine kernels.

STRAWBERRIES

'Doubtless God could have made a better berry,' said Yeats, 'but doubtless God never did.' The strong flavour of strawberry is best on its own. Strawberries are at their peak in June and July. It is no accident that Wimbledon is associated with strawberries. That's when the outdoor crop peaks. But farmers have extended the local season. They grow berries in poly-tunnels, which ripen as early as mid-April, and ever-bearing varieties provide a steady crop from mid-June to October. The latter are usually raised in Growbags. They are difficult to grow organically.

A strawberry should be dense and juicy, red to the core, fragrant, and sweet. Most imports are mealy, hollow, and bland. Even when they are locally grown, supermarket varieties such as *Elsanta* are ordinary. Try *Tamella, Korona* or *Pegasus*. *Totem* keeps its shape and texture when frozen. *Tri-star* is one of the sweeter ever-bearing types. *Wild Alpine* strawberries, or *fraises de bois*, are small, red or cream-coloured, especially fragrant, and prized for flavour. They are rarely cultivated for sale because yields are low and they are very soft when ripe.

A perfectly ripe strawberry is firm, almost crisp. It should slice easily. Whether you are picking your own or buying at market, white-tipped berries are fine, even preferable. They'll ripen within a day, while a ripe strawberry begins to go mushy and ferment in the same period. An overripe berry is purple, not red, and dull, not shiny. The strawberry's flavour deteriorates rapidly after peak ripeness.

Why do fresh berries at market, picked yesterday, often spoil faster than older, imported berries in the shops? The supermarket berries are picked less ripe. They also receive pre- and post-harvest chemicals to inhibit spoilage. If you find farmers who don't use these chemicals, support them.

The strawberry's classic partner is rhubarb, at its peak in May and June. Italians sprinkle fine balsamic vinegar on sliced berries. Black pepper and fresh orange juice are also nice.

SEASON

Outdoor main crop: late June and early July. Early poly-tunnel crop: from mid-April. Ever-bearing varieties: from mid-June to October.

WHAT TO LOOK FOR

Dry, shiny berries, no bruises, lively green caps. Tips can be white or pink; they'll ripen nicely in one day. Size and shape don't matter. Taste one.

STORAGE

Perishable. Put unwashed fruit in one layer on kitchen towels, in a cool, shady place, and eat within 2 days. To make berries last longer, cut in half and sprinkle with sugar. Add to muffins, fruit salad, pancakes or porridge.

MAKING THE MOST OF A SURPLUS

Smoothies. Jam and syrup keep and freeze well. Quickest freezing: wash, pat dry, hull, freeze whole on a tray, and transfer to plastic bags. Frozen sugared berries are better: cut in half, sprinkle with sugar, leave for 20 minutes to draw out the juices and freeze in even quantities.

STRAWBERRY GRANITA

Granita is sorbet with a rougher texture – the kind you get when you do not use an ice-cream maker. The more you stir it while it freezes, the smoother it will be, because you stop ice crystals forming. Alcohol lowers the freezing temperature, allowing it to be slushy.

SERVES 4–6

500 ml Strawberry Jam (see opposite)
100 ml fruit wine, such as raspberry
   or cherry, or fruity grape wine
   such as Gamay

- Purée the jam in a food-processor until it is completely smooth. Add the wine and blend again.
- Freeze in an ice-cream maker according to the instructions, or in a wide, shallow dish. Every so often, stir or poke it with a whisk, fork, or potato masher. You can even reblend it in the food-processor.
- The more you stir the better, but I have frozen it for 2 hours, stirred only once, and served it.
- If you don't plan to eat it straight away, transfer it to a small, covered container and freeze. Allow it to soften in the fridge for 20–30 minutes before eating.

QUICK STRAWBERRY JAM & SYRUP

Easy, and keeps in the fridge for several weeks. Otherwise you can sterilise and seal the jars properly and eat strawberry jam in January. The lazy way is to freeze it. Making your own pectin is easy, but shop-bought is fine.

MAKES about 1 litre jam

1.5 kg strawberries, hulled

300 g sugar

150 ml Pectin (see p. 219)

1–4 tsp lemon juice (to taste)

- Cut the large strawberries in half. Leave the small ones whole but crush them slightly. A whole berry in jam is wonderful.
- Add the sugar, mix well, and leave the berries to release their juice, about 2 hours.
- Put the pectin and strawberries into a large uncovered saucepan. Bring them to the boil, then simmer for 20–25 minutes, stirring often, until the bubbles are small and shiny. Add more sugar to taste.
- For strawberry syrup, strain now and eat the fruit pieces on toast.
- The jam will be ready when a spoonful cools to form a skin. If, after 25 minutes, it does not, add a splash more pectin and lemon juice and cook a bit longer. Or not.

Variation: This basic jam recipe works with blueberries and raspberries. The berries can be mixed. Blueberries are high in pectin and can be added to thicken it. Currants and gooseberries contain more pectin; reduce the quantity given above by half.

STRAWBERRY SHORTCAKE

On the farm, we eat this twice a week in strawberry season. It is best hot, but is also nice cold, for breakfast. The shortcake itself is like scones, but fluffier. The acidic yoghurt helps them rise. If you can find skimmed buttermilk, even better: use 400 ml in place of the milk and yoghurt.

SERVES 8–10

1.5 kg strawberries, washed, hulled, and halved

6 tbsp Vanilla Sugar (see p. 19)

600 g flour

2 tbsps sugar

3 tbsp baking powder

½ tsp salt

125 g chilled butter

300 ml milk

100 ml yoghurt (or 400 ml skimmed buttermilk)

ice cream or whipped cream

- Pre-heat oven to 230°C.
- Mix the strawberries with the vanilla sugar and set aside to allow the sugar to extract the juice. A syrup will form.
- Make the shortcake: mix all the dry ingredients, except a handful of flour, by sifting or whisking in a large bowl. With a pastry blender or two knives – or your fingers – cut in the butter until the mixture is like coarse meal. Bits of butter should be pea-sized or smaller. Later it melts, leaving air pockets for fluffy biscuits.
- Add the milk and yoghurt and mix quickly to a soft dough. Do not overwork it, or the shortcake will be tough. It should be no more than three minutes from now to baking.
- Pat the dough into a circle ½ cm thick on a lightly floured cool surface. Cut it with a biscuit cutter or upside-down glass about 4–5 cm wide. Place the circles close together, like honeycombs, in a buttered baking pan.
- Bake for 15–20 minutes, until puffy and slightly brown on the edges.
- Split open a shortcake in a bowl and top it with strawberries and juice. Serve with whipped cream or ice cream.

Variation: Replace strawberries with Stewed Rhubarb (see p. 183).

SWEDE, TURNIPS & KOHLRABI

These *brassica* family vegetables aren't fashionable. Many Europeans survived on swede during the Second World War, so its association with privation is strong. Turnips are animal fodder, and no one's heard of the tender kohlrabi. If some television chef took up its cause, it would probably become the new rocket.

Before the New World potato arrived, the turnip and parsnip were Europe's staple starches. Turnips are yellow or white, sometimes with green or purple shoulders where the root was above ground and exposed to light. Raw, they taste of mustard like their hotter cousin, the radish. Turnips are not very dense and cook quickly. Roasted, they are almost sweet, and they add a peppery bite to potato latkes. There is no need to peel a turnip, and young ones can be eaten whole. Turnips are a bit sweeter after a light frost.

The slightly prickly turnip tops are another dark leaf green to savour. They are rich in vitamins A, B and C, calcium, and potassium. Cook in very little water and dress them with olive oil and vinegar. In the American South they cook the greens with bacon. In May, turnip greens with small new bulbs, such as *Early Snowball*, appear at market. Slice the root, chop the greens, and sauté both in olive oil, roots first, then leaves.

Swede is related to the turnip. It is a large, round, yellow and purple root. The yellow or white flesh of swede is more delicate than that of carrot, less sweet than parsnip, not as sharp as a turnip, and delicious roasted with all three. It is lovely puréed with potatoes and an apple. Swedes are denser than turnips and take longer to cook.

Wild cabbage and turnip are the ancestors of kohlrabi, a swollen stem that grows above ground. It is an orange-sized globe with pale green, purple, or white skin, and slender stems emerging from all sides, shooting straight up. Kohlrabi is tender, with the faint taste of radish. There's no need to peel young ones. Kohlrabi can be eaten raw as a crudité. It is nice steamed until crisp-tender and dressed with olive oil, or in a warm salad with something sweet, like a pear.

SEASON

Swede: from October, from storage until February. Turnips: June to November. Kohlrabi: June to September.

WHAT TO LOOK FOR

Firm, unblemished skin, heavy for their size. No grey mottled patches, which are caused by frost. Turnip tops and kohlrabi stems should be fresh, not wilted.

STORAGE

Unwashed, tops cut off, in a plastic bag as cool as 0°C. The refrigerator is fine. Use swedes within 3–4 weeks, turnips in 2 weeks and kohlrabi in a week.

MAKING THE MOST OF A SURPLUS

Turnip soup and swede purée. These don't freeze well.

SAUTÉED BABY TURNIPS & CARROTS

Strong winter vegetables taste better when immature than summer ones, which are mostly water. A tiny courgette has very little flavour, but a little turnip is tangy. You can leave them whole, and they are pretty.

3 baby turnips per person, trimmed

3 baby carrots per person, trimmed

5 baby leeks per person, white part only
  (finger-sized)

1 tbsp olive oil per person

- Bring salted water to the boil, blanch the carrots and turnips until just short of crisp-tender. Drain.
- Sauté the leeks in the olive oil. When they are half done, add the root vegetables and sauté until they are golden and the leeks are soft, with brown edges. Season to taste.

KOHLRABI & PEAR SALAD WITH CHIVES

1 kohlrabi per person, peeled

1 firm pear such as *Concord* per person

2 tsp chopped chives and chive flowers
  (or parsley) per person

2 tsp olive oil per person

- Bring to the boil 4 cm salted water, just enough to cover the kohlrabi. Meanwhile, peel the kohlrabi. Slice it in rounds, and then into sticks about 1 cm thick. Cook in 2 cm water until tender but not mushy. Drain and keep warm in saucepan.
- Cut the pears into similar matchstick-shaped pieces. Mix together all the ingredients gently, and season to taste. Serve warm, or at room temperature.

ROASTED TURNIP PURÉE

There is no need to peel a turnip. The skin is tender and full of vitamins.

SERVES 2–4

500 g turnips, trimmed and chopped

1 yellow onion, peeled and chopped

2 tbsp olive oil

- Set the oven to 180°C. Chop turnips and onions, mix with 1 tbsp olive oil, and salt lightly. Roast until completely soft and slightly brown on the edges, about 30 minutes.
- Purée everything with 1 tbsp olive oil. Salt and pepper to taste.

SWEETCORN

It used to be gospel: you must eat sweetcorn the day it is picked, preferably within hours. From the moment it is picked, its sugars begin to turn to starch. In just 6 hours at room temperature, corn loses up to 40 per cent of its sugars. Sweetcorn is still best within hours of picking, but two new kinds have helped matters: 'sugar-enhanced' varieties convert sugar to starch more slowly and stay tender longer, and the gene in 'super-sweet' varieties makes them exceptionally sweet – too sweet for some.

Sweetcorn goes starchy faster when it is hot and dry. Farmers should pick in the early morning when the ears are cool from the previous night. Sweetcorn should be kept cool and moist, in wet baskets or sheets, at market. Do not allow it to get hot on the way home.

Yellow sweetcorn is most common in Britain, but it may also be white, bi-coloured, and even red. Bi-colour has mixed white and yellow kernels and tastes much like yellow. White sweetcorn is sometimes sweeter than yellow corn, but it has less corn flavour than yellow or bi-colour. *Sweet Nugget* and *Challenger* are super-sweets; *Tuxedo* and *Champ* sugar-enhanced.

American Indians taught the colonists to plant corn and beans together, and to mix them in a dish called succotash. Americans eat succotash at Thanksgiving, which celebrates a probably apocryphal feast the Pilgrims threw for the Indians. It is a simple sauté of equal parts corn and lima or butter beans and a little parsley. If you can't eat corn on the cob the day you buy it, it is still fine for cornbread, soups, and stir-fries.

SEASON

August, September, and early October.

WHAT TO LOOK FOR

Tight, green husk, with fresh 'flags', the green ribbon-like leaves. The top of the silk is brown and dry. The fresher the stem end, the better. Ear heavy for its size, evenly filled out from stem to tip. Ask when it was picked.

STORAGE

If the corn was sitting in the sun at market or got hot on the way home, dunk it in cold water for a minute to cool it. Keep it in a plastic bag in the fridge, with the leaves moist. Shuck just before cooking. Flavour and tenderness fade after 1–2 days.

MAKING THE MOST OF A SURPLUS

Corn freezes beautifully. Stand ear in a wide, shallow pan and slice down with a serrated knife, getting as much kernel as possible without hitting the cob. Freeze kernels in plastic bags.

CORN ON THE COB

1–2 ears sweetcorn per person

1 tsp parsley, chives, dill, tarragon or basil,
  finely chopped

1 tsp melted butter or olive oil per ear

- Boil lots of salted water and cook the corn for 3–4 minutes. The fresher it is, the less cooking it needs.
- Blend the herbs with the butter or oil and serve with the hot corn and lots of salt and pepper.

Variations: Garlic-in-Oil (see p. 219) or Chilli Oil (see p. 153) are delicious with sweetcorn too.

PLUM & ROASTED SWEETCORN SALSA

The boxy little **Habanero** *is the hottest chilli.* **Scotch Bonnet** *is a good substitute; both are fruity and go well with tropical dishes. If the plums are not very ripe or juicy, add a bit of honey or apple juice. Eat it with blue maize tortilla chips or shredded chicken stuffed in pitta.*

SERVES 6-8

4 ears sweetcorn, husks and silk removed

1 tbsp olive oil (for corn)

1/2 red onion

1/2–3/4 *Habanero* or *Scotch Bonnet*,
  finely chopped, seeds removed

8 ripe Victoria plums, halved

1/2 orange bell pepper, cut in strips

1 tsp best olive oil (for salsa)

1 tsp honey or 1 tbsp apple juice
  (both optional)

- Heat the grill. Rub olive oil and salt all over the ears of corn.
- Grill for about 40 minutes, turning every 10 minutes as the kernels turn brown. When the kernels are soft, cut them off the cob, leaving the tough white part on the ear but getting all the flesh.
- Dice the onion and chilli in a food-processor. Add the plums and sweet pepper in chunks, pulsing briefly until they are pea-sized.
- Mix with the corn, olive oil, honey or apple juice if using, and salt to taste. This tastes even better the next day.

CHILLI CORNBREAD

Cornbread is easy, quick, and amenable to variation. It can be sweet or savoury, dry or moist, light or rich. For a different texture, try fine or coarse polenta. Raw, cooked, and frozen sweetcorn work. There is no need to defrost frozen sweetcorn before using.

SERVES 8–10

250 g sweetcorn kernels

200 g polenta

175 g plain flour

1 tbsp baking powder

³/₄ tsp salt

2 tbsp olive oil, or melted butter

350 ml milk (or half yoghurt, half milk)

2 tbsp honey

2 eggs

¹/₂–1 red chilli pepper or 1 green *Jalapeño*, finely chopped, or 1–1¹/₂ tsp red pepper flakes

oil for frying-pan

- A 28-cm ovenproof frying-pan is best for a crispy crust, but a baking tin works. If your frying pan is smaller, bake any excess batter in a tin.
- Set the oven to 200°C.
- Mix the dry ingredients well.
- If you want the heat of the chilli suffused throughout the cornbread instead of in little bites, soak the chilli in the olive oil for 20 minutes.
- Whisk the wet ingredients, then add the corn and chillies.
- Oil the pan and heat it in the oven until it is sizzling. This makes a crispy crust.
- Pour the wet mixture into the polenta and stir in quickly. Ignore the odd lump: overbeating makes tough cornbread.
- Pour it into the hot pan. Bake for 25–30 minutes, until the top is golden, the sides are brown, and a cocktail stick comes out clean. Serve hot with butter or honey, or eat with black bean chilli, tomato soup or greens, such as mustard, dressed with oil.

Variations: To the basic recipe (no corn or chillies), add 4 tablespoons of honey or pure maple syrup, smoked bacon, sautéed onion, or grated cheddar. More polenta (225 g) and less flour (150 g) makes a coarser bread. Another 50 ml of milk makes it moister.

TOMATOES

At the farm, we grow all kinds of vegetables, but some 25 different varieties of tomatoes are the cash crop and kitchen staple. Tomatoes are everyone's favourite vegetable. My mother says they are better than fruit. Anatomically, the tomato *is* a fruit. Like dessert fruits, it must ripen properly for optimum eating. At the farmers' market you should find tomatoes prized for flavour and texture, not for their tough skin and long shelf-life.

It is well known that many supermarket tomatoes are picked green and hard. Those showing a tinge of pink are plucked out for 'vine-ripened' and the rest go into cold storage. Often, ethylene gas is piped in to ripen the fruit. The result is a hard, pale, tasteless tomato. But ethylene itself is not responsible for lousy supermarket tomatoes. The greatest sins against flavour are poor-tasting varieties, removing the tomato too soon from its source of nourishment (the vine), and cold storage.

Some fruits, like apples, must ripen on the tree. Others, like pears, must be picked under-ripe for perfection. The tomato falls in between. It must begin to ripen on the plant, but a half-ripe tomato ripens beautifully at room temperature. As with wine, the tomato flavour is a balance between sweetness and acidity. During ripening, both acids and sugars increase, sugars more so.

Never refrigerate tomatoes, even ripe ones. The cold destroys their texture and flavonoids, the compounds responsible for flavour. Never ripen tomatoes in the window. They must be out of the sun, and the window sill can be cold at night.

Tomatoes come in two types. The first sort are tall vine or indeterminate plants. They flower and fruit indefinitely, until frost. Determinate tomatoes are compact and produce a finite number of flowers and fruit. In general, indeterminate varieties taste better. They include the exceptionally sweet cherry tomato and many old-fashioned heritage varieties.

A few superior-tasting varieties: *Marmande, Brandywine,* and *Costuluto Florentino* (beefsteaks); *Ailsa Craig, St. Pierre,* and *Harbinger; Tigerella* (small with gold stripes); *Mirabelle, Sweet 100,* and *Sungold* (yellow, red, and orange cherry tomatoes); *San Marzano* (thick-walled plum type for sauces). Ask your farmers to grow them.

SEASON

Peak season: July to September (including glasshouse tomatoes, June–November).

WHAT TO LOOK FOR

Heavy fruit, no cracks in the stem end. Half-ripes are convenient for the cook, as they ripen over the week.

STORAGE

Between 13 and 24°C, out of the sun. Never refrigerate. To ripen faster, put in a closed paper bag with a banana, which traps ethylene gas. A ripe tomato is delicious for about a week. Eat cherry tomatoes within a day or two.

MAKING THE MOST OF A SURPLUS

Sauce and Passata freeze well (see p. 215).

POACHED SALMON WITH TOMATOES & ROCK SALT

An easy summer lunch from my friend Angus MacKinnon. The salt should be crunchy. Flakes also work. If you do not have fish stock, use water.

500 ml mixture of white wine, light fish stock, and water (to cover fish)

1 bay leaf

rock salt

2 tsp best olive oil per person
+ a little extra

1 salmon fillet per person

1 large tomato per person

1 handful basil per person

- In a heavy pan bring the stock to the boil with the bay leaf, a little salt, and a drizzle of olive oil. Add the salmon, bring the pan back to the boil, cover it, turn off the heat, and leave it on the burner.
- While the salmon is poaching, dice the tomatoes, shred the basil, and toss them in the oil.
- When the salmon is just pink in the centre, lift it out with a slotted spoon, put it on plates and top with the tomatoes. Sprinkle liberally with rock salt.

Variation: Use 1 large handful of cherry tomatoes per person, cut in half. Or use yellow pear tomatoes.

PANZANELLA

This Italian bread salad is a meal in itself.

SERVES 6

2 cloves garlic, crushed, peeled, and finely chopped

4 tbsp red wine vinegar

1 kg ripe tomatoes, seeded and chopped, juice reserved

4 tbsp best olive oil

1 cucumber, seeded and chopped

1½ loaves day-old white bread, preferably Italian, such as ciabatta

25 basil leaves, cut in strips

1 small jar dried, salt-packed capers, rinsed and drained

1 small jar dried, salt-packed anchovies, rinsed and drained

- In a mortar and pestle, make a dressing with the garlic, vinegar, tomato juice, and oil. Or chop all ingredients as finely as possible and mash them together.
- Tear the bread into bite-sized chunks and toast it lightly. Put it into a salad bowl and toss it in the dressing. Add the cucumbers, tomatoes, and basil. Scatter over the capers and anchovies and marinate for at least 1 hour. Season to taste and eat at room temperature.

BAKED TOMATOES
WITH WALNUT PESTO

The garlic stays raw – if you do not like it, leave it out.

100 g basil, leaves only

25 g walnuts

1 large clove garlic, peeled

50 ml olive oil

1 large or 2 medium tomatoes per person

- Heat the grill. Process basil, garlic, walnuts, and olive oil to a rough paste. Salt to taste.
- Cut a cap off each tomato, opposite the stem end. Scoop out the seeds and pulp. Stuff the tomato with pesto, replace the cap, and brush the skin with olive oil.
- Grill for 10 minutes, until the flesh is cooked and the skin is peeling back. The pesto should be warm through, but still bright green. Serve warm.

CLASSIC SALSA CRUDA

Salsa is on the table in Mexican households at every meal. Unless you are very certain of chillies, put in half, taste, then add the rest. Eat with Fajitas (see p. 152), bean burritos, or blue maize tortilla chips.

SERVES 2– 4

400 g ripe tomatoes

50–100 ml water

1/2 white onion

1 *Cayenne* or 2 *Serrano* or *Jalapeño* peppers

3 tbsp fresh coriander

1/4–1/2 tsp salt

- Put half of the tomatoes, 50 ml of the water, and all the other ingredients into the food-processor and purée until mostly smooth. The tomatoes and onions should be lentil-sized.
- Taste for salt and heat, then adjust the seasoning and chill. Dice the remaining tomatoes finely and add. If the tomatoes are not very juicy, add another 50 ml of water.
- Eat immediately as it tends to get watery.

Variation: Add 1 clove garlic.

OVEN-DRIED TOMATOES

1 kg ripe tomatoes

2 tbsp olive oil

salt

- Set the oven to 125°C.
- Leave cherry tomatoes whole. Halve or quarter larger ones. Put tomatoes of equal size in each baking tin.
- Roll the tomatoes in oil and salt and put them in one layer in a baking tin. Bake for 3–8 hours and remove when they are ready. After 3 hours, smaller tomatoes are ready for a mozzarella sandwich, still a bit juicy. After 8 hours, they are leathery and intensely flavoured.
- Packed in oil, they keep for a week to 10 days in the fridge or a cool pantry.

Ways to eat dried tomatoes, packed in oil or not

Add to minestrone, lentil soup, or cannellini beans simmering in their juice with garlic. Set the tomatoes on Baked Polenta (see p. 219). They are good in sandwiches spread with soft cheese, or on pasta, pizza, crostini, bruschetta, and salads. When cherry tomatoes are still juicy and hot, toss them with pasta, olive oil, and basil.

The longer the tomatoes sit in the oil, the tastier both become. Strained, the reddish oil is wonderful on bread and salads. Or whiz 1–2 tomatoes with their oil for a more intense flavour. Optional: add 1 clove of garlic or 1 anchovy per 3 tablespoons of oil.

ROCKET, DRIED TOMATOES & GOAT'S CHEESE

SERVES 4

5 tbsp Oven-dried Tomato oil (see above)

2 tbsp red wine vinegar

10–12 Oven-dried Tomatoes, depending on size (see above)

salt and pepper

125 g rocket

1 shallot, finely chopped

50–75 g soft goat's cheese, to taste

- In a large jar, shake together the oil, vinegar, and tomatoes. Season them. Put them in a bowl with the rocket and shallot, and crumble over the goat's cheese. Toss everything. This salad can sit for a bit. Eat it at room temperature.

SAUCES

For sauce, thick-fleshed plum tomatoes are better than juicy slicing tomatoes. Peeled and seeded tomatoes are indispensable for perfectly smooth sauce, although I often leave in the seeds and skin. Pasta sauce, especially tomato and cream-based, tends to thicken off the heat. Pasta also absorbs sauce as soon as you toss it. Both can make pasta dry when you bring it to the table. Three tricks to keep it glistening and moist: do not overdrain pasta; add a ladle or two of cooking water as you toss it with the sauce; and dress the pasta just before you eat it. The sauce should coat the pasta thinly – no puddles.

HOW TO PEEL AND SEED TOMATOES

- Boil a large pan of water. Fill a large bowl with cold water.
- Cut an X in the skin on the blossom end (opposite the stem). Drop tomatoes in batches into the boiling water for 30 seconds.
- Remove them with a slotted spoon and put them in the cold water. When they are cool, peel back the skin, cut out the stem and scoop out the seeds.

SUMMER TOMATO SAUCE

SERVES 4

2 tbsp Garlic-in-Oil (see p. 219)

1 kg ripe tomatoes, peeled, seeded,
  and chopped (see above)

25 basil leaves, sliced into strips

2 tsp honey (optional – how sweet are
  the tomatoes?)

¼ tsp ground cayenne (optional)

½ tsp salt

- Heat the garlic and oil gently in a heavy saucepan for 2 minutes. Add the tomatoes and the basil, then simmer for about 20 minutes. Half-way through, taste and add cayenne, honey, and salt.
- You can purée the sauce or leave it chunky.

PASSATA

This plain Italian tomato sauce comes bottled, often with basil. It is cheap and handy. It is also easy to make and a great way to use up tomatoes. A good substitute is a tin of tomatoes run through a hand-cranked food mill or mouli, with a little of their juice.

1.5 kg tomatoes, peeled and seeded
  (see opposite)
20 basil leaves, chopped (optional)

• Boil the tomatoes and a little salt until soft and mushy. Add the basil when the passata is nearly ready. Pass through a mouli. Keeps for a week or two in the fridge and freezes well.

THICK TOMATO SAUCE WITH DRIED TOMATOES

An all-pantry, no-shopping meal. Optional non-perishable additions: black olives, chick peas, anchovies, capers or dried **shiitake** *mushrooms (soaked in water first).*

SERVES 4

½ yellow onion, chopped fine
3 tbsp Garlic-in-Oil (see p. 219)
1 tsp dried oregano or basil

3 x 400-g tins tomatoes, chopped
12–16 Oven-dried Tomatoes (see p. 213)
½ tsp salt

• Sauté the onion, Garlic-in-Oil, and oregano. Add the tinned tomatoes and cook for 5 minutes.
• Chop the dried tomatoes into bite-sized pieces. Add to the sauce and cook until it is of the desired thickness, about 15 minutes. Season to taste. To suffuse the sauce with the meaty flavour of dried tomato, you can purée it.

UNCOOKED TOMATO SAUCE

SERVES 4

6 ripe, best-tasting tomatoes, diced
4 cloves garlic, smashed, peeled, and finely chopped
about 20 basil leaves, chopped
2 tbsp best olive oil

• Mix together all the ingredients and let the sauce sit for 4–8 hours in a cool place.
• Toss it with hot spaghetti and season to taste. Leftovers make a garlicky salsa.

GAZPACHO

In most restaurants Gazpacho is like a smooth salsa – delicious, but not very Andalucian. The real thing is silky and pink, made with bread and no green vegetables. Add chillies little by little unless you are very sure of the heat. Pass round bowls of diced cucumbers, red and green peppers, hard-boiled egg, and spring onion.

SERVES 4

1 mild green *Jalapeño* or 1 hot red
  Cayenne chilli (to taste)

1 kg ripe tomatoes, chopped

1 small white onion, chopped

2–4 cloves garlic, smashed and peeled,
  to taste

2 tbsp olive oil

3 slices thick white bread, crusts removed

1 tbsp white wine vinegar

200–250 ml cold water

1/4 tsp paprika

1/4 tsp salt

For the garnishes

1 small cucumber, dried

1 medium red pepper, dried

2 spring onions, chopped

2 hard-boiled eggs, crumbled

• Chop the chilli, discarding the seeds and pith. Purée all the ingredients until completely smooth.

SWORDFISH WITH QUICK & CHUNKY TOMATO SAUCE

SERVES 2

2 pieces swordfish

juice of 1 lemon

1 tbsp + 1 tsp olive oil

2 cloves garlic, thinly sliced

2 tomatoes, diced but not peeled

1 tbsp balsamic vinegar

1 tbsp chopped parsley

• Marinate the fish in the lemon juice, 1 teaspoon of olive oil, salt, and pepper.
• Sauté the garlic and parsley until they are soft. Do not let them brown.
• Add the vinegar and the tomatoes. Stir, cover, and simmer until the tomatoes are soft. Season.
• In a clean pan, fry the swordfish on both sides and top with sauce.

BASIC RECIPES

MAYONNAISE

I am a fan of the food-processor, but with mayonnaise, a whisk and bowl give you more control. Whisking is less work if the bowl is deep and narrow.

Mayonnaise is an emulsion: a mixture of such fine particles that it becomes a new, third substance. If the yolk and oil do not form an emulsion, it stays thin, gloopy, and dark yellow. It should turn pale yellow and form stiff peaks. You will whisk without stopping for about 20 minutes. If the mayonnaise does not take, crack a new yolk in a clean bowl, and add the un-emulsified mixture to the yolk drip by drip, as if it were new oil.

Some recipes call for 500 ml of oil – the yolks will take it, if you are patient – but I like the consistency, flavour, and quantity with 250 ml. If you do not like the taste of olive oil, use sunflower oil.

One batch makes about 8 tablespoons, enough for about 8 people on asparagus, or to dress at least 2 large salads. Use within 7 days.

2 egg yolks at room temperature
250 ml best olive oil
¹/₂ juice lemon

- In a bowl, whisk the yolks until they are smooth. Add the oil by half a teaspoonful at a time, whisking all the while. Do not add more oil until the mayonnaise has set. It will turn a shade paler yellow than the yolks and begin to thicken.
- Proceed cautiously for at least 10 minutes, adding oil little by little. You can add the oil faster in the last few minutes.
- Add the lemon juice and salt and pepper to taste. If you do not like the look of black pepper, use white.

Variation: Add ¹/₂–1 tsp of Dijon mustard.

BASIL MAYONNAISE

- You can make a rough herb mayonnaise by finely chopping the herbs, but if you add a smooth herb purée, like a pesto, the end product has more flavour.
- Once the mayonnaise is set, reserve about 2 tablespoons of oil. In a blender, purée it with 15–20 basil leaves.
- Mix it well with the mayonnaise and season as above.

Variations: Blend 1 clove of garlic, crushed and peeled, with the pesto, or use 3–4 tablespoons of tarragon leaves in place of the basil.

AÏOLI – GARLIC MAYONNAISE

A classic Provençal dressing. Delicious in salad Niçoise. In Spain it is served with paella.

- Crush, peel, and finely chop 1–4 cloves of garlic to taste, and mash well with 2 tablespoons of oil in a blender or mortar and pestle. The more violently you pound it, the stronger the taste of garlic. Mix well with the basic mayonnaise.

SHORTCRUST PASTRY

It is worth becoming expert at your own pastry recipe. If you do not have a food-processor, cut the butter into small pieces, then rub it into the flour with your fingers. For savoury recipes, omit the sugar. The pastry can be frozen in a flattened disc.

This recipe is enough for one pie with 2 crusts, one top and one bottom in a 22–25-cm tin.

300 g flour	**¹/₂ tsp salt**
1–2 tbsp vanilla sugar	**200 g butter**
3–4 tbsp ice water	

- Chill all the ingredients for at least 30 minutes.
- Mix the dry ingredients with a sifter or whisk and put them into the food-processor.
- Cut the butter into small pieces; add it to the flour and process, using the pulse button, in 3-second bursts until the butter pieces are about the size of lentils. Do not overdo it.
- Add the ice water a spoonful at a time, pulsing briefly. Once you have added the butter and water, work the dough as little as possible, for not more than 30 seconds. Squeeze it between your fingers; when it sticks to itself, turn it on to a piece of clingfilm and form it into a roundish lump. Flatten it into a thick disc, 3–4 cm thick, wrap it well, and refrigerate for 1 hour.
- You can make it a day ahead.
- Cut the pastry disc in half and roll out each crust on a flat, floured surface with a floured rolling-pin and hands. Rolling-pin and surface should be cool, or the butter in the pastry melts. You can roll the dough between parchment paper or clingfilm. Roll it from the centre out, in rays.
- For a blind-baked crust: lay the pastry in the tin, poke a few holes in the bottom with a fork, cover it with foil, weighed down with dried beans or a smaller tin, and bake at 200°C for about 10 minutes.
- Remove the foil and continue to bake for 5–7 minutes. Then take it out of the oven and allow it to cool. It can be frozen.

CUSTARD

Unless you are very patient, make custard in a bain-marie or double-boiler. Put 4–5 cm water in a large pan, bring it to the boil, set the smaller saucepan over the water and then turn down the heat and simmer. Stir the custard constantly. Do not let it boil. If it turns grainy, it has begun to curdle and there is no undoing it. Custard thickens a little once it is off the heat. The vanilla makes little black specks. If you don't like them, do not split the pod, but the flavour will not be as strong.

SERVES 4

500 ml milk	**1 vanilla pod**
5 egg yolks	**80 g vanilla sugar**

- Put the milk in a saucepan, split the vanilla pod lengthways, and scrape its seeds into the milk. Add the pod, and warm the milk until just before it boils. If there is time, leave it to infuse for 30 minutes.
- Whisk the yolks and sugar into a smooth paste. Pour the warm (not hot) milk over the eggs and mix well.
- Heat the custard slowly in a clean pan over the water bath, stirring constantly, for about 20 minutes, until it thickens.
- Serve warm or cool. Cover and refrigerate it.

EASY PIZZA CRUST

It really is easy, and it freezes well. Remember to leave time for rising. Some of the flour is for kneading. You may not use all of it.

MAKES two 30-cm crusts, each serving 6–8

250 ml warm water	**1 tsp honey or sugar**
1 scant tbsp dried yeast	**1 tbsp olive oil**
¹/₂ tsp salt	**400–450 g plain flour**

- Put the water into a large bowl. Dissolve in it the honey or sugar, then stir in the yeast. Let the mixture stand until it is bubbly, 5–15 minutes. Hot water kills yeast.
- Add the oil, salt, and about 400 g of the flour, and form the mixture into a ball that pulls away from the sides of the bowl.
- Turn the dough on to a floured surface and knead it for a full 5 minutes, or longer, until the dough is firm, smooth, elastic, and not sticky.
- Put it into a clean, oiled bowl. Rub a bit of oil over all sides of the dough, cover it with a towel, and leave it in a warm, draught-free place until it has doubled in bulk. This takes at least 30 minutes; an hour is fine. (Now prepare the topping.)
- When the dough has risen, set the oven to 240°C. Punch down the dough, divide it in half, and make it into 2 smooth balls. (Here freeze one or both crusts.)
- Unless you are an Italian whiz, you will not be able to toss pizza dough to stretch it. A reasonably good method: flatten the ball into a circle as big as your open hand with fingers splayed. Lift the disc and hold it before you like a clock on the wall. Move the pizza anticlockwise, forming a thicker edge with your thumb and forefingers. The weight of the dough will stretch the disc evenly. If it tears, repair it later. Rotate it as many times as you can, then lay the disc on a baking sheet or pizza stone, which you have sprinkled with oil. The edge can be thick or thin, as you wish. Another cheat: use a rolling-pin, as with pastry.
- Add the toppings and cook until the dough is crispy, about 20 minutes.

POLENTA

Like pizza, polenta is easy to make and dress up. It is also wholesome and filling. Polenta is ground dried maize, usually yellow.

Keep polenta in the freezer: the oils in whole grains go rancid once ground and exposed to the air. It will stay fresher for longer.

Polenta is hearty and bland. You need to add moisture, fat, and flavour. It is served three ways: wet (soft and moist, with a topping such as sautéed oyster mushrooms); baked (firmer, usually in wedges); or grilled (cooled, sliced, buttered or oiled, and grilled).

All these forms begin with the basic recipe, which serves 8–10.

2 litres water
1¹/₂ tsp salt
300 g polenta

- Boil the salted water in a large saucepan.
- In a thin stream, pour in the polenta, stirring fast. Keep pouring in spurts, stirring well in between, until the mixture is smooth.
- Reduce the heat and cook for about 40 minutes. Stir often and vigorously, scraping the bottom and sides of the pan. It should be soft and thick, and taste cooked.
- To serve it wet: dish it up as soon as it is cooked, with toppings such as grated cheese, stewed meat or sautéed mushrooms.

Variations: cook it with half milk or chicken stock to enrich it; or stir in 1–2 tablespoons oil, butter or Parmesan when it is still hot, just before topping.

- To serve it baked: spread the hot polenta in a dish, add the toppings, such as a blob of pesto mixed with goat's cheese, and bake at 190°C for about 20 minutes. Cool slightly (or completely) to set. Slice in squares or wedges.
- To serve it grilled: spread the wet polenta on a flat sheet in a rectangular shape about 5 cm thick, as evenly as you can. Let it cool completely. Make long, 2-cm thick slices across the rectangle or squares. Brush with oil or butter and grill in a ridged pan or grill.

PECTIN

Most fruits contain some pectin, which gives jams a smooth, semi-solid consistency. Pectin is easily extracted by boiling apples (even cores and peel will do) or lemon slices, with the yellow peel pared off, leaving the white pith.

MAKES about 600 ml, enough for 4 jam recipes

1.5 kg Bramleys or other cooking apple
1.5 litres water

- Chop the unpeeled apples into quarters, keeping the core.
- Put them into a large saucepan with the water and bring it to the boil, then reduce the heat and simmer for 25 minutes until the apples collapse. Let it cool.
- Gather the apples in a muslin cloth over a strainer and drain for 12 hours or overnight. Do not squeeze.
- Discard the apples and reduce the liquid by half.
- Refrigerate it and use it within 5 days, or freeze in 150-ml batches.

BASIC PASTRY CREAM

This is rich. It makes about 500 ml, a thick layer of custard for a 22-cm tart, or a thin layer for two tarts.

6 egg yolks	**100 g vanilla sugar**
100 g flour	**500 ml milk**
pinch of salt	**1 tbsp natural vanilla extract**
1 tbsp butter	

- In a heavy saucepan, whisk together the yolks and sugar until the mixture is thick and light yellow.
- Add the flour bit by bit, sifting it through a sieve and stirring briskly.
- In a separate pan, heat the milk. Add it gradually to the egg mixture, stirring constantly.
- When it is very smooth, add the vanilla and a pinch of salt.
- Heat gently in a double-boiler, whisking constantly until it starts to thicken. Then stir it quickly to stop lumps forming. It should mound nicely on the spoon. Stir in the butter and remove the pan from the heat. Allow it to cool, covered tightly with clingfilm touching the top of the custard to stop a skin forming.

FISH, CHICKEN, & VEGETABLE STOCK

Stock is easy, quick, flexible, and freezes well. There is no need to follow the recipe exactly. About 1.5 kg vegetables to 800 ml water gives you about 500 ml stock, a useful quantity.

For all stocks:
- Quarter but do not peel the vegetables. Smash but do not peel the garlic.
- Use 2 bay leaves, a few peppercorns, and any other fresh herbs to hand, such as thyme or parsley, in whole sprigs. Use strong herbs like rosemary and sage sparingly.
- Heat and stir vegetables, herbs, and any bones in 1–2 tablespoons of olive oil until aromatic. A big splash of white wine is nice.
- Add 1 litre of cold water, boil, and simmer uncovered until vegetables and bones give up their flavour, about 20 minutes for fish and vegetables, 1–2 hours for meat. Simmer only. Do not boil.
- Strain. Do not add salt, or you will salt the final dish twice. To make it stronger, reduce the stock further, now or later.

Vegetable. Some vegetables are too strong (the broccoli family turns sulphurous); some stain the stock (beetroots); and some are too good for stock (whole asparagus – use just the ends). Summer vegetables like courgettes and French beans consist mostly of water and are too bland. Potatoes, pumpkins, and winter squashes (with seeds and peel), fennel, mushrooms, carrots, onions, leeks, garlic, and celery are good. For all-purpose stock, do not let any one vegetable dominate.

Fish. Some say to use only white flaky fish, not oily ones, but I use salmon heads. They are cheap if not free at the fishmonger and make a strong stock. Use one or two fish heads and some other bones and scraps such as lobster bodies, prawn shells and heads, or last night's whole fish. Salvage flavour wherever you can: save poaching liquid to begin building a stock. Keep vegetable flavours simple. Onion and garlic and perhaps one herb, such as thyme, is plenty.

Chicken, beef, veal, lamb. Use the carcass of a roast, or ask the butcher for stock bones and cuts. For pure meat flavour, skip vegetables. Instead of sautéing, brown the bones in the oven but do not let them burn. To remove the fat, cool the stock overnight and skim off the hardened fat.

GARLIC-IN-OIL

Chop several cloves of garlic, cover them with olive oil and keep them in a jar in the fridge. Use the garlic or oil or both as needed, and add more of both. In a week, start a fresh jar.

WHAT'S IN SEASON?

During 'Peak Season', produce is at its best and most likely to be at the farmers' market. Because of storage and season-extending methods such as poly-tunnels, some produce may be available earlier or later. For more detail, see each section.

	PEAK SEASON		PEAK SEASON
APPLES	SEPTEMBER – DECEMBER	KALE	SEPTEMBER – MARCH
ASIAN GREENS	SEPTEMBER – MAY	KOHLRABI	JUNE – SEPTEMBER
ASPARAGUS	APRIL – JUNE	LEEKS	SEPTEMBER – APRIL
AUBERGINE	JULY – SEPTEMBER	LETTUCE	MAY – OCTOBER
BEANS		MUSHROOMS	ALL YEAR
BROAD	JUNE – JULY	PARSNIPS	SEPTEMBER – DECEMBER
FRENCH	JULY – SEPTEMBER	PEARS	SEPTEMBER – OCTOBER
RUNNER	JUNE – OCTOBER	PEAS	
BEETROOT	JUNE – NOVEMBER	SHELL	JUNE – AUGUST
BLACKBERRIES	JULY – SEPTEMBER	MANGETOUT	JUNE – AUGUST
BLUEBERRIES	JULY – AUGUST	SUGAR SNAPS	JULY – AUGUST
BROCCOLI		PEPPERS	AUGUST – OCTOBER
PURPLE SPROUTING	FEBRUARY – APRIL	PLUMS	AUGUST – SEPTEMBER
HEADED	JUNE – NOVEMBER	POTATOES	MAY – NOVEMBER
BRUSSELS SPROUTS	SEPTEMBER – MARCH	PUMPKINS	SEPTEMBER – NOVEMBER
CABBAGE	SEPTEMBER – APRIL	RADISHES	APRIL – NOVEMBER
CARROTS	JUNE – OCTOBER	RHUBARB	FEBRUARY – MAY
CAULIFLOWER	ALL YEAR	ONIONS	JULY – OCTOBER
CAVOLO NERO	AUGUST – DECEMBER	RASPBERRIES	JUNE – SEPTEMBER
CELERIAC	SEPTEMBER – DECEMBER	SHALLOTS	AUGUST – DECEMBER
CELERY	JULY – DECEMBER	SPINACH	MAY – NOVEMBER
CHERRIES	JULY	SPRING GREENS	JANUARY – APRIL
COURGETTES	JUNE – OCTOBER	SPRING ONIONS	MARCH – DECEMBER
CUCUMBERS	JUNE – SEPTEMBER	STRAWBERRIES	JUNE – JULY
CURRANTS	JUNE – AUGUST	SUMMER SQUASH	JUNE – OCTOBER
FENNEL	JULY – SEPTEMBER	SWEDE	SEPTEMBER – DECEMBER
GARLIC	JULY – NOVEMBER	SWEETCORN	AUGUST – OCTOBER
GOOSEBERRIES	JUNE – AUGUST	SWISS CHARD	JUNE – NOVEMBER
HERBS		TOMATOES	JULY – OCTOBER
ANNUALS	JULY – SEPTEMBER	TURNIPS	JUNE – NOVEMBER
PERENNIALS	ALL YEAR	WATERCRESS	MARCH – OCTOBER
JERUSALEM ARTICHOKE	OCTOBER – FEBRUARY	WINTER SQUASH	OCTOBER – DECEMBER

WEIGHTS & MEASURES

All recipes have been tested using metric weights and measures,
and a standard non-convection oven.

1 teaspoon = 5 ml,   1 tablespoon = 15 ml.   Spoons are measured level.

If you prefer to use imperial weights and measures, you can use the following table as a
guide. However, note that conversions suggested here are not exact equivalents, and that
metric and imperial measurements should not be used together in the same recipe.

WEIGHTS		VOLUME MEASURES		LINEAR MEASURES	
15 g	($\frac{1}{2}$ oz)	75 ml	($2\frac{1}{2}$ fl oz)	3 mm	($\frac{1}{8}$ in)
30 g	(1 oz)	90 ml	(3 fl oz)	5 mm	($\frac{1}{4}$ in)
55 g	(2 oz)	100 ml	($3\frac{1}{2}$ fl oz)	1 cm	($\frac{1}{2}$ in)
85 g	(3 oz)	120 ml	(4 fl oz)	2 cm	($\frac{3}{4}$ in)
100 g	($3\frac{1}{2}$ oz)	150 ml	(5 fl oz)	2.5 cm	(1 in)
115 g	(4 oz)	200 ml	(7 fl oz)	5 cm	(2 in)
140 g	(5 oz)	250 ml	($8\frac{1}{2}$ fl oz)	7.5 cm	(3 in)
170 g	(6 oz)	300 ml	(10 fl oz)	10 cm	(4 in)
200 g	(7 oz)	360 ml	(12 fl oz)	15 cm	(6 in)
225 g	(8 oz)	400 ml	(14 fl oz)	20 cm	(8 in)
300 g	($10\frac{1}{2}$ oz)	450 ml	(15 fl oz)	25 cm	(10 in)
340 g	(12 oz)	500 ml	(17 fl oz)	30 cm	(12 in)
400 g	(14 oz)	600 ml	(1 pint)		
450 g	(1 lb)	750 ml	($1\frac{1}{4}$ pints)		
500 g	(1 lb 2 oz)	900 ml	($1\frac{1}{2}$ pints)		
550 g	($1\frac{1}{4}$ lb)	1 litre	($1\frac{3}{4}$ pints)		
600 g	(1 lb 5 oz)	1.2 litres	(2 pints)		
675 g	($1\frac{1}{2}$ lb)	1.5 litres	($2\frac{3}{4}$ pints)		
750 g	(1 lb 10 oz)	2 litres	($3\frac{1}{2}$ pints)		
800 g	($1\frac{3}{4}$ lb)				
900 g	(2 lb)				
1 kg	($2\frac{1}{4}$ lb)				
1.25 kg	($2\frac{3}{4}$ lb)				
1.5 kg	(3 lb 3 oz)				
2 kg	($4\frac{1}{2}$ lb)				

INDEX